INTRODUCING
ISSUES WITH
OPPOSING
VIEWPOINTS®

Sexual Orientation

Lauri S. Scherer, *Book Editor*

GREENHAVEN PRESS
A part of Gale, Cengage Learning

GALE
CENGAGE Learning·

Detroit • New York • San Francisco • New Haven, Conn • Waterville, Maine • London

Elizabeth Des Chenes, *Director, Publishing Solutions*

© 2013 Greenhaven Press, a part of Gale, Cengage Learning

Gale and Greenhaven Press are registered trademarks used herein under license.

For more information, contact:
Greenhaven Press
27500 Drake Rd.
Farmington Hills, MI 48331-3535
Or you can visit our Internet site at gale.cengage.com

For product information and technology assistance, contact us at

Gale Customer Support, 1-800-877-4253
For permission to use material from this text or product, submit all requests online at
www.cengage.com/permissions

Further permissions questions can be e-mailed to permissionrequest@cengage.com

Articles in Greenhaven Press anthologies are often edited for length to meet page requirements. In addition, original titles of these works are changed to clearly present the main thesis and to explicitly indicate the author's opinion. Every effort is made to ensure that Greenhaven Press accurately reflects the original intent of the authors. Every effort has been made to trace the owners of copyrighted material.

Cover image © Rikke/Shutterstock.com

LIBRARY OF CONGRESS CATALOGING-IN-PUBLICATION DATA

Sexual orientation / Lauri S. Scherer, book editor.
   p. cm. -- (Introducing issues with opposing viewpoints)
  Includes bibliographical references and index.
  ISBN 978-0-7377-6281-5 (hbk.)
  1. Sexual orientation--Juvenile literature. 2. Homosexuality--Juvenile
literature. I. Scherer, Lauri S.
  HQ18.5.S49 2012
  306.76--dc23

           2012009957

Printed in the United States of America
1 2 3 4 5 6 7 16 15 14 13 12

Contents

Chapter 3: What Laws Should Be Made Regarding Sexual Orientation?

Foreword

Indulging in a wide spectrum of ideas, beliefs, and perspectives is a critical cornerstone of democracy. After all, it is often debates over differences of opinion, such as whether to legalize abortion, how to treat prisoners, or when to enact the death penalty, that shape our society and drive it forward. Such diversity of thought is frequently regarded as the hallmark of a healthy and civilized culture. As the Reverend Clifford Schutjer of the First Congregational Church in Mansfield, Ohio, declared in a 2001 sermon, "Surrounding oneself with only like-minded people, restricting what we listen to or read only to what we find agreeable is irresponsible. Refusing to entertain doubts once we make up our minds is a subtle but deadly form of arrogance." With this advice in mind, Introducing Issues with Opposing Viewpoints books aim to open readers' minds to the critically divergent views that comprise our world's most important debates.

Introducing Issues with Opposing Viewpoints simplifies for students the enormous and often overwhelming mass of material now available via print and electronic media. Collected in every volume is an array of opinions that captures the essence of a particular controversy or topic. Introducing Issues with Opposing Viewpoints books embody the spirit of nineteenth-century journalist Charles A. Dana's axiom: "Fight for your opinions, but do not believe that they contain the whole truth, or the only truth." Absorbing such contrasting opinions teaches students to analyze the strength of an argument and compare it to its opposition. From this process readers can inform and strengthen their own opinions, or be exposed to new information that will change their minds. Introducing Issues with Opposing Viewpoints is a mosaic of different voices. The authors are statesmen, pundits, academics, journalists, corporations, and ordinary people who have felt compelled to share their experiences and ideas in a public forum. Their words have been collected from newspapers, journals, books, speeches, interviews, and the Internet, the fastest growing body of opinionated material in the world.

Introducing Issues with Opposing Viewpoints shares many of the well-known features of its critically acclaimed parent series, Opposing Viewpoints. The articles are presented in a pro/con format, allowing readers to absorb divergent perspectives side by side. Active reading questions preface each viewpoint, requiring the student to approach the material thoughtfully and carefully. Useful charts, graphs, and cartoons supplement each article. A thorough introduction provides readers with crucial background on an issue. An annotated bibliography points the reader toward articles, books, and websites that contain additional information on the topic. An appendix of organizations to contact contains a wide variety of charities, nonprofit organizations, political groups, and private enterprises that each hold a position on the issue at hand. Finally, a comprehensive index allows readers to locate content quickly and efficiently.

Introducing Issues with Opposing Viewpoints is also significantly different from Opposing Viewpoints. As the series title implies, its presentation will help introduce students to the concept of opposing viewpoints and learn to use this material to aid in critical writing and debate. The series' four-color, accessible format makes the books attractive and inviting to readers of all levels. In addition, each viewpoint has been carefully edited to maximize a reader's understanding of the content. Short but thorough viewpoints capture the essence of an argument. A substantial, thought-provoking essay question placed at the end of each viewpoint asks the student to further investigate the issues raised in the viewpoint, compare and contrast two authors' arguments, or consider how one might go about forming an opinion on the topic at hand. Each viewpoint contains sidebars that include at-a-glance information and handy statistics. A Facts About section located in the back of the book further supplies students with relevant facts and figures.

Following in the tradition of the Opposing Viewpoints series, Greenhaven Press continues to provide readers with invaluable exposure to the controversial issues that shape our world. As John Stuart Mill once wrote: "The only way in which a human being can make some approach to knowing the whole of a subject is by hearing what can be said about it by persons of every variety of opinion and studying all modes in which it can be looked at by every character of mind. No wise man ever acquired his wisdom in any mode but this." It is to this principle that Introducing Issues with Opposing Viewpoints books are dedicated.

Introduction

On September 19, 2011, fourteen-year-old Jamey Rodemeyer, a gay teen from Buffalo, New York, ended his life. Rodemeyer killed himself after enduring countless gay slurs and death wishes from classmates and anonymous strangers online. "JAMIE IS STUPID, GAY, FAT ANND UGLY. HE MUST DIE!" wrote one nameless poster to the website Formspring. Another person wrote, "I wouldn't care if you died. No one would. So just do it :) It would make everyone WAY more happier!"[1]

Jamie Hubley, a gay fifteen-year-old from Ottawa, Canada, met a similar end a month later. Hubley struggled with depression and loneliness, and he was the target of bullies who tormented him for his sexuality. He chronicled his struggles on a blog. In his last post before his death in October 2011, it was clear he had lost hope his life would improve. "Im sorry, I cant take it anymore," he wrote. "Being sad is sad :/. I'v been like this for way to long. I cant stand school, I cant stand earth, I cant stand society. How do you even know It will get better? Its not. . . . Remember me as a Unicorn :3 x) MAybe in my next life Il be a flying squirreel :D . . . Il fly away."[2] Hubley's father, Ottawa city councilor Allan Hubley, told reporters that his son tried to start a gay-straight alliance club at his school, but classmates tore down his posters and called him hurtful, cruel names in the hallways and on the Internet.

Hubley and Rodemeyer are joined by Eric James Borges, Tyler Clementi, Billy Lucas, Asher Brown, Seth Walsh, Justin Aaberg, and other gay youth who have killed themselves when their sexuality has tragically intersected with bullying, rejection by their families, depression, mental illness, and social isolation. These issues make gay teens two to three more times likely to commit suicide than their straight counterparts, according to the civil rights organization Lambda Legal.

Although statistics on the problem are hard to come by, one study published in a 2006 issue of the *Journal of Adolescent Health* found that 52 percent of gay and bisexual teen boys had attempted suicide, compared to 13 percent of straight teen boys. For people like Dan Savage, these statistics show that gay teens need extra support and resources. This is why in 2010, Savage, with the help of his partner, created the It Gets Better Project, in which adults post inspirational videos for lesbian, gay, bisexual, and transgendered children struggling with coming out, bullying, and other issues. "The point of the 'It Gets Better' project is to give kids like Jamey Rodemeyer hope for their futures," said Savage after Rodemeyer's suicide. "But sometimes hope isn't enough. Sometimes the damage done by hate and by haters is simply too great. Sometimes the future seems too remote. And those are the times our hearts break."[3] Savage has been joined by Neil Patrick Harris, Ellen DeGeneres, Secretary of State Hillary Clinton, and Harvard Law School professor Elizabeth Warren, all of whom have filmed their own "It Gets Better" videos.

Yet not everyone agrees that gay teens are more at risk for suicide, and some challenge the notion that gay teen suicides constitute a crisis or epidemic. Skeptics include conservative Peter LaBarbera, who dismisses claims that gay teen suicides occur as the result of bullying or social isolation. "Homosexuality is a condition—apart from societal acceptance or nonacceptance—that often leads to unhealthy behavior, which leads to unhappiness,"[4] which in turn leads to suicide, says LaBarbera. LaBarbera is president of the group Americans for Truth about Homosexuality (AFTAH), which is dedicated to exposing what it calls the "homosexual activist agenda." LaBarbera claims that gay activists have hijacked the issue of teen suicide in an attempt to push their political agenda.

Ritch Savin Williams, professor of developmental psychology at Cornell University, also rejects the notion that there is a gay suicide epidemic. Williams has studied the lives of gay teens and concludes, "90 percent are actually doing quite well. They are not depressed. They are not anxious. They're not attempting suicide. They're really quite ordinary adolescents." Williams argues that gay teens are just as healthy, strong, and positive as their straight counterparts. He worries that sending gay youth the message that they are somehow more fragile or susceptible to suicide than straight teens is damaging to them. "From a scientific perspective, there is certainly no gay suicide epidemic," he told National Public Radio in 2010. "But the more problematic aspect for me is that I worry a great deal about the image that we are giving gay-identified youth."[5]

Whether there is a gay teen suicide crisis and how to support at-risk gay and lesbian youth are among the many issues discussed in *Introducing Issues with Opposing Viewpoints: Sexual Orientation.* Readers will also consider arguments about whether gay marriage should be legalized, how schools should handle sexual orientation, whether sexual orientation is chosen, and more. Guided reading questions and essay prompts will help students articulate their own opinions on this important and relevant topic.

Notes

1. Quoted in Susan Donaldson James, "Gay Buffalo Teen Commits Suicide on Eve of National Bullying Summit," ABCNews.com, September 21, 2011. http://abcnews.go.com/Health/gay-buffalo -teen-commits-suicide-eve-national-bullying/story?id=14571861# .TyBN8phoqi4.
2. Quoted in *Huffington Post*, "Jamie Hubley, Gay 15-Year-Old Ottawa, Canada, Teen Commits Suicide, Cites Depression, School Troubles," October 17, 2011. www.huffingtonpost .com/2011/10/17/jamie-hubley-commits-suicide_n_1015646 .html.
3. Quoted in Lucas Grimley, "Jamey Rodemeyer, 14, Dies in Suicide," *Advocate*, September 21, 2011. www.advocate.com/News/Daily _News/2011/09/20/Jamey_Rodemeyer_14_Dies_in_Suicide.
4. Peter LaBarbera, "The Gay Youth Suicide Myth," *Orthodoxy Today*. www.orthodoxytoday.org/articles/LabarberaSuicideMyth.php.5.
5. Quoted in Robert Siegel, "A Look at the Lives of Gay Teens," National Public Radio, October 21, 2010. www.npr.org/templates /story/story.php?storyId=130732158.

Chapter 1

What Is the Nature of Sexual Orientation?

Controversy has long raged over whether a person's sexual orientation is chosen or innate.

Viewpoint

1

Sexual Orientation Is Chosen

Michael Medved

"Homosexual activity appears to represent a passing phase, or even a fleeting episode, rather than an unshakable, genetically predetermined orientation."

In the following viewpoint, Michael Medved argues that choice and circumstances play a role in whether a person identifies as homosexual. He discusses a 2011 study, which found that fewer Americans identify themselves as gay than previously thought. Medved argues the study's results show that people outgrow homosexual periods in their life; experiment with sexuality; and make other choices that indicate homosexuality is, for some, a phase that they choose to enter and exit. Medved says nothing is wrong with this—many other pieces of identity are chosen and still deserve respect. He concludes that sexual orientation is more likely to involve choice than the gay community would like the rest of America to believe.

Medved is the host of a nationally syndicated talk radio show and the author of *The 5 Big Lies About American Business*. He contributes to *USA Today*, where this viewpoint was originally published.

AS YOU READ, CONSIDER THE FOLLOWING QUESTIONS:
1. What percentage of the population identifies as homosexual, according to the National Center for Health Statistics and the Centers for Disease Control and Prevention?
2. Why, according to Medved, has the phrase "sexual preference" been replaced with the term "sexual orientation"?
3. What do religious identity and sexual orientation have in common, according to the author?

The nation's increasingly visible and influential gay community embraces the notion of sexual orientation as an innate, immutable characteristic, like left-handedness or eye color. But a major federal sex survey suggests a far more fluid, varied life experience for those who acknowledge same-sex attraction.

The results of this scientific research shouldn't undermine the hard-won respect recently achieved by gay Americans, but they do suggest that choice and change play larger roles in sexual identity than commonly assumed.

Choice Plays a Role in Sexual Identity

The prestigious study in question (released in March [2011] by the National Center for Health Statistics [NCHS] and the Centers for Disease Control and Prevention [CDC]) discovered a much smaller number of "gays, lesbians and homosexuals" than generally reported by the news media. While pop-culture frequently cites the figure of one in 10 (based on 60-year-old, widely discredited conclusions from pioneering sex researcher Alfred Kinsey) the new study finds only 1.4% of the population identifying with same-sex orientation.

Moreover, even among those who describe themselves as homosexual or bisexual (a grand total of 3.7% of the 18–44 age group), overwhelming majorities (81%) say they've experienced sex with partners of the opposite gender. Among those who call themselves heterosexual, on the other hand, only a tiny minority (6%) ever engaged in physical intimacy of any kind with a member of the same sex. These figures indicate that 94% of those living heterosexual lives felt no physical attraction to members of the same sex, but the great bulk of self-identified homosexuals and bisexuals feel enough intimate interest in the opposite gender to engage in erotic contact at some stage in their development.

Sexual Orientation Is Often a Phase

Gay pride advocates applaud the courage of those who "come out," discovering their true nature as homosexual after many years of heterosexual experience. But enlightened opinion denies a similar possibility of change in the other direction, deriding anyone who claims straight

The author argues that choice and circumstance play a role in whether a person identifies as homosexual.

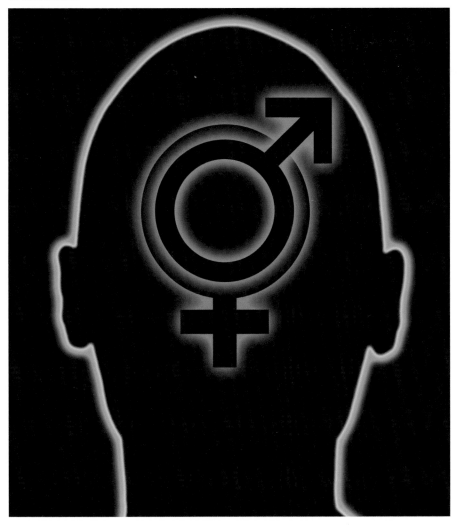

orientation after even the briefest interlude of homosexual behavior and insisting they are phony and self-deluding. By this logic, heterosexual orientation among those with past gay relationships is always the product of repression and denial, but homosexual commitment after a straight background is invariably natural and healthy. In fact, numbers show huge majorities of those who "ever had same sex sexual contact" do not identify long-term as gay. Among women 18–44, for instance, 12.5% report some form of same sex contact at some point in their lives, but among the older segment of that group (35–44), only 0.7% identify as homosexual and 1.1% as bisexual.

In other words, for the minority who may have experimented with gay relationships at some juncture in their lives, well over 80% explicitly renounced homosexual (or even bisexual) self-identification by age of 35. For the clear majority of males (as well as women) who report gay encounters, homosexual activity appears to represent a passing phase, or even a fleeting episode, rather than an unshakable, genetically predetermined orientation.

> **FAST FACT**
>
> A 2010 study published in the *Journal of Biosocial Science* reported that gay and lesbian parents are more likely to have gay, lesbian, bisexual, or unsure (of sexual orientation) sons and daughters. Percentages of children of gay and lesbian parents who were not heterosexual ranged between 16 percent and 57 percent.

The once popular phrase "sexual preference" has been indignantly replaced with the term "sexual orientation" because political correctness now insists there is no factor of willfulness or volition in the development of erotic identity. This may well be the case for the 94% of males and 87% of females (ages 18–44) who have never experienced same-sex contact of any kind and may never have questioned their unwavering straight outlook—an outlook deemed "normal" in an earlier age.

Fewer Gays than Previously Thought

For the less than 2% of men and women who see themselves as gay, however, the issue of sexual orientation remains vastly more complicated. Within a month of the release of the CDC/NCHS report, one of the world's most respected think tanks on gay life confirmed some of its most surprising findings, without specifically referencing the recent government study. UCLA's Williams Institute on Sexual Orientation Law and Public Policy offered a new estimate of homosexual identification: concluding that 1.7% of Americans say they're gay, and a slightly larger group (1.8%) identified as bisexual—by definition attracted to both genders and shaping their sexual behavior through some mixture of inclination and preference.

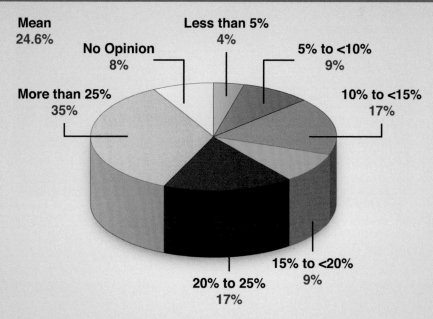

Americans Vastly Overestimate How Many People Are Gay

US adults, on average, estimate that 25 percent of Americans are gay or lesbian, despite the fact that most research puts the actual figure between 1 and 5 percent.

Just your best guess, what percentage of Americans today would you say are gay or lesbian?

Mean
24.6%

No Opinion
8%

More than 25%
35%

Less than 5%
4%

5% to <10%
9%

10% to <15%
17%

15% to <20%
9%

20% to 25%
17%

Red numbers represent the percentage of respondents having each opinion.
All figures are approximate.

Taken from: Gallup Organization, May 5–8, 2011.

Brad Sears of the Williams Institute defended the accuracy of these numbers, suggesting gay leaders "let go" of previous, unrealistic estimates of homosexual orientation. He told the Associated Press that "with other populations of a similar size of 2% to 4%, we don't question whether there are too many or too few." For instance, no one suggests Jewish Americans should be treated with contempt or dismissed as irrelevant to the Christian majority because they number below 2% of the U.S. population. Nor would the news media shy away from reporting that in an age of religious conversion choice plays a role in adding to and subtracting from the Jewish community.

Sexuality Has an Element of Choice

Religious identity arises from birth, upbringing, instinct, even destiny, but the fact that it almost always includes some element of choice doesn't entitle the believer to less respect. By the same token, it's no sign of hostility or homophobia to point to recent data suggesting that life experience and personal decisions play roles alongside inborn inclination in the complex, sometimes inconclusive, emergence of the gay and lesbian identity.

> ## EVALUATING THE AUTHOR'S ARGUMENTS:
>
> Michael Medved argues that for many people, choice, age, and life circumstance affect whether a person identifies as homosexual. In the following viewpoint, the Liberty Education Forum argues that sexuality is determined at an early age or even before birth. After reading both viewpoints, with which author do you agree, and why? List at least two pieces of evidence that swayed you.

Sexual Orientation Is Not Chosen

Liberty Education Forum

"Biology, not choice, drives sexual orientation— both gay and straight."

The Liberty Education Forum (LEF) is a nonprofit organization that works to achieve liberty, freedom, and fairness for all Americans, regardless of their sexual orientation. The forum supports a number of gay rights issues, including the ability of gays to serve openly in the military, their right to marry, and their right to bear and adopt children.

In the following viewpoint, the LEF argues that sexual orientation is not chosen. Rather, the organization frames it as an innate biological trait, similar to left-handedness or other traits determined at or before birth. It highlights the findings of a number of studies that show sexuality to be influenced by genetics, hormones, and brain development. The LEF says that when people understand sexual orientation as something biologically determined rather than chosen, they are more likely to support equal rights for gay people. Therefore, the LEF concludes that myths about sexuality and choice hurt the gay community.

Liberty Education Forum online, "Executive Summary; Genetic Evidence; Hormonal Influences; Brain Structure and Organization," 2008. http://libertyeducationforum.org. Copyright © 2008 by Liberty Education Forum. All rights reserved. Reproduced by permission.

AS YOU READ, CONSIDER THE FOLLOWING QUESTIONS:
1. What is the heritability of sexual orientation, according to the LEF? How does this compare to left-handedness?
2. What is androgen and how does it affect sexuality, according to the LEF?
3. What is the anterior hypothalamus and how does it affect sexuality, as reported in the viewpoint?

The discussion about sexual orientation remains on center stage in the public arena as Americans debate how to treat gay and lesbian people. From the halls of state legislatures to the chambers of supreme courts; from the desks of city councils to the federal government in Washington, DC; and from the pews of churches to the dinner tables of ordinary families, citizens everywhere are confronting the question about how to treat the small minority of citizens who are gay or lesbian.

FAST FACT

An April 2011 study released by the Williams Institute at the University of California School of Law found that more than 8 million American adults—about 3.5 percent of the total population—identify as lesbian, gay, or bisexual.

An Inborn Trait

As author Chandler Burr said in our first white paper on the subject, "The raging debate about gay rights ultimately turns on one simple question—is homosexuality a lifestyle choice or is homosexuality an inborn biological trait? Put another way, does someone choose to be gay or are they just born that way?" As the following pages illustrate, we already know the answer to this question. This is an important question in the gay rights debate. If people understand that sexual orientation is an inborn trait, they are much more likely to support fairness and equal rights for gay people.

Overwhelming evidence indicates an innate nature to sexual orientation. Numerous scientific studies are indisputable. Research into

Americans' Views on Sexual Orientation

The majority of Americans believe that gays and lesbians cannot change their sexual orientation.

Can sexual orientation be changed?

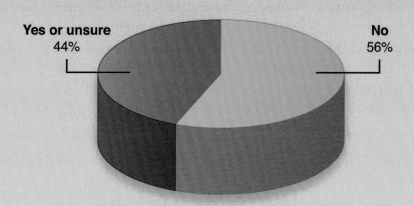

Yes or unsure
44%

No
56%

What contributes to the development of sexual orientation?

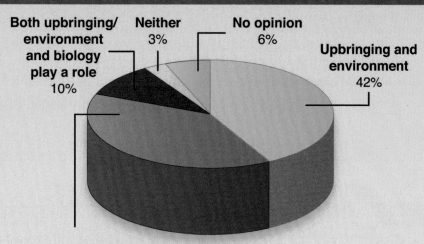

Both upbringing/
environment
and biology
play a role
10%

Neither
3%

No opinion
6%

Upbringing and
environment
42%

Sexual orientation is something
people are born with
39%

Taken from: CNN/Opinion Research Corporation poll, June 27, 2007.

the origins of human sexual orientation proves beyond any reasonable doubt that people do not choose their sexual orientation. Scientists don't yet know the exact origins, but they know that it's not chosen.

Science Shows Sexuality Is Innate

In these pages, we [the Library Education Forum] have attempted to provide an accurate summary of the known scientific evidence on this issue:

Genetic Evidence—The best evidence right now is that genetics play a significant but not determinative role in sexual orientation, and in this respect, it is similar to many traits affecting a minority of the population. Sexual orientation, as a trait, is similar to being left or right-handed; the genetic influence on both traits is estimated at less than 50%; and both seem to be established at an early age or before birth.

Hormonal Influences—There is evidence that hormonal influences in the mother's womb affect the sexual orientation of a child. One researcher finds a prenatal origin to sexual orientation. To put it simply, something was happening in the wombs of the mothers he studied to influence the sexual orientation of their later sons.

Brain Structure and Organization—Scientific findings strongly indicate that the brain structure of heterosexuals is different from homosexuals. Gay men's object location memory skills, for instance, exceed that of straight men. . . .

Genetic Evidence

- Sexual orientation has a strong physiological component. It appears to be influenced by both genetic and hormonal factors.
- The trait is similar to being left or right-handed; the genetic influence on both traits is estimated at less than 50%; and both seem to be established at an early age or before birth.
- A same-sex orientation is held by approximately 3–5% of the world's population. There are twice as many homosexual males as females.
- Sexual orientation is a complex trait which appears to have multiple mechanisms acting upon it. It is unlikely that there is a single cause, although it is quite clear that the primary roots of the trait lie in biology.

- There is evidence of a pattern of maternal transmission for male homosexuality (for it being "passed down" by unknown means through the mother's side of the family).
- The heritability of sexual orientation is estimated between 30% and 50%. By comparison, the heritability of left-handedness is estimated at 26% or lower.

According to the author, genetics and hormones as well as brain structure and organization play a role in determining sexual orientation.

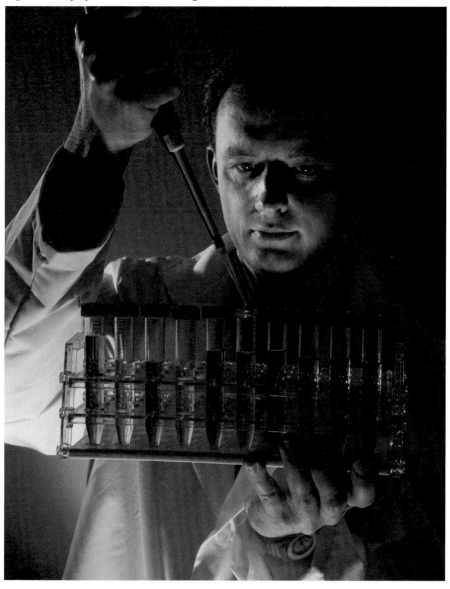

- Significant genetic linkage to male homosexuality has been found on the X Chromosome at Xq28 and on Chromosome 7 at 7q36, with two additional regions (8p12 and 10q26) identified as areas of interest for future study.
- Male identical twins are more likely than non-identical twins or ordinary siblings to share the same sexual orientation. Siblings are more likely to share the same orientation than non-siblings.
- The sexual orientation of adopted children is not influenced by that of their adoptive parents, which points to biology rather than upbringing as the defining influence. . . .

Hormonal Influences
- There is evidence in many lesbian and bisexual females of brain structures that have been partially masculinized by exposure to high levels of the male hormone androgen before birth.
- There is evidence that prenatal androgen plays more of a role in homosexuality in women than it does in men.
- Manipulating prenatal hormone levels has been shown to alter sexual orientation in laboratory mice and in sheep. . . .

Brain Structure and Organization
- Gay men and lesbians are more likely than straight men and women to be left-handed. Since hand preference can be observed in the womb, this suggests a prenatal influence.
- Gay men's object location memory skills exceed that of straight men. Gay men's skill level in this involuntary indicator of brain organization between the sexes approaches that of straight women.
- Both lesbians and gay men outperform heterosexual men and women in verbal fluency from early childhood.
- There is strong evidence that the structure of the anterior hypothalamus in mammals influences sexual orientation in males.
- A small group of cells in the anterior hypothalamus known to be involved in the generation of male-typical sex behavior in animals is, on average, smaller in gay men than in straight men. The same area in sheep is smaller in male rams that mate exclusively with other rams than it is in "straight" rams.
- PET Scans show that the brains of gay men and lesbians process some scents differently than straight men and women; a clear difference in an involuntary brain process. . . .

A Matter of Biology, Not Choice

Science is firmly on the path of establishing the innate nature of the trait of homosexuality. The preponderance of the evidence would lead any rational person to conclude that biology, not choice, drives sexual orientation—both gay and straight.

EVALUATING THE AUTHOR'S ARGUMENTS:

The Liberty Education Forum suggests that when people understand sexual orientation as something biologically determined rather than chosen, they are more likely to support equal rights for gay people. Why do you think this might be true? Suggest two reasons.

It Should Not Matter Whether Sexual Orientation Is Chosen

Greta Christina

"When I hear people defend gay rights by saying, 'Of course it's not a choice, who would choose to be queer?' . . . My reaction is to raise my hand and say, 'Me. Over here. I would.'"

In the following viewpoint, Greta Christina argues that whether gay people choose their sexuality is irrelevant to whether they deserve rights. She says that just because someone is born a certain way does not make them more privy to rights, respect, or equality. Likewise, choosing to live a particular lifestyle does not mean someone forfeits their rights. She resents people trying to show the innateness of homosexuality by saying that no one would choose to be gay. She loves her life and who she is, and although she did not choose her sexuality, she would not trade her life for anyone else's. She concludes that whether sexuality is a choice should not factor into debates about gay rights, because choice has no bearing on rights.

Christina is a prolific writer about gay and lesbian issues, atheism, politics, culture, and other subjects. Her articles have appeared in *Ms.*, the *Chicago Sun-Times*, *Skeptical Inquirer*, and on AlterNet.org, where this viewpoint was originally published.

AS YOU READ, CONSIDER THE FOLLOWING QUESTIONS:
1. How has choice factored into Christina's relationships?
2. What does the phrase "load the dice" mean in the context of the viewpoint?
3. What is a pedophile, and how does this topic factor into Christina's argument?

In the various and sundry debates about gay rights, the question of whether sexual orientation is a choice comes up with almost irritating predictability. And when it does, one of the things I've noticed is that bisexuality—as it so often does—gets completely ignored. So I want to talk a little about bisexuality, sexual orientation, and choice.

Because, speaking as a bisexual person, in my experience I do have something of a choice.

The Element of Choice in Relationships

Of course it's true that I don't have a choice about who I'm sexually attracted to. And I didn't have a choice about who I fell in love with. I don't choose that, any more than anyone else does. But back when I was dating, I did have a choice about who I dated and who I socialized with. At the time that I fell for Ingrid, I was dating women, and socializing in the lesbian community, a whole lot more than I was with men and in the hetero community. And I was doing it out of choice.

On the whole, I like women more than men. Sexually I like both roughly the same (with something of a preference for women on the whole, but with that preference varying a lot over the years). But personally, emotionally, I tend to like women better than men. Not as friends necessarily—I have plenty of male friends—but as romantic partners. The personality traits that, in my experience, women tend to have more than men—cooperation, empathy, emotional expressiveness, good listening skills, yada yada yada—are traits that I like, and traits that I find central to a good relationship.

Attitudes about sexual orientation have changed significantly since 1973. In that year, just 10.7 percent of Americans thought homosexuality was not wrong at all, compared to more than 40 percent in 2010. Other surveys and studies have found higher support for gay rights when people believe homosexuality is an innate trait, rather than something chosen.

Year	Always Wrong	Almost Always	Sometimes Wrong	Not Wrong at All	Don't Know, etc.
1973	69.7%	6.5%	7.4%	10.7%	5.8%
1974	66.1%	5.3%	8.1%	12.3%	8.2%
1976	67.1%	6.0%	7.6%	14.8%	4.4%
1977	69.4%	5.6%	7.2%	13.1%	4.9%
1980	70.6%	5.8%	5.7%	13.6%	4.4%
1982	71.0%	4.8%	6.2%	13.5%	4.5%
1984	72.1%	4.3%	6.8%	12.8%	4.0%
1985	73.3%	4.0%	6.8%	12.7%	3.2%
1987	75.0%	4.0%	6.1%	11.6%	3.3%
1988	74.6%	4.3%	5.3%	12.2%	3.6%
1989	70.8%	3.8%	6.0%	14.6%	4.8%
1990	72.8%	4.7%	5.5%	12.3%	4.7%
1991	72.1%	3.5%	3.7%	13.8%	6.8%
1993	62.2%	3.9%	7.3%	20.7%	6.0%
1994	63.7%	3.5%	5.5%	21.5%	5.8%
1996	56.6%	4.7%	5.5%	25.9%	7.3%
1998	54.3%	5.5%	6.8%	26.2%	7.2%
2000	53.7%	4.1%	7.4%	26.4%	8.4%
2002	53.5%	4.9%	7.1%	30.4%	4.1%
2004	56.4%	4.7%	6.7%	29.1%	3.1%
2006	53.4%	4.6%	6.4%	30.7%	5.1%
2008	49.2%	2.9%	6.3%	35.5%	6.2%
2010	43.5%	3.4%	7.5%	40.6%	4.9%

Taken from: General Social Survey, NORC/University of Chicago, September 2011.

Now, of course, that's a generalization, and a very broad one at that. Not all women are like that, and plenty of men are. And if I'd happened to meet and fall for a man who was cooperative and empathetic and expressive and a good listener etc., then that would have been just ducky. But back when I was dating, dating women just seemed to make more sense. It was the smart way of playing the odds. It was loading the dice.

And it works the other way, too. I've known other bisexuals who date and socialize more heterosexually—again out of choice.

"I'd Still Choose to Be Queer"

Whatever It is, IMO [in my opinion] one of the differences between being bisexual and being monosexual (hetero- or homosexual) [sic]. You can, in theory, be happy being sexual and romantic with someone of either gender . . . and so you have at least some degree of choice about which gender you get involved with. Indeed, if your relationship preference is very strong indeed, you can actually flat-out refuse to get involved with potential partners of one gender or the other, even if your libido or your heart is temporarily pulling you towards them . . . and unlike homosexual people who refuse to accept their homosexuality, you can still have a happy and satisfying sexual and romantic life. And even if you don't go that far, you can still generally date and socialize with the gender and the community you'd prefer to end up with. You can't choose who you get the hots for . . . but you can hang out with the kind of people you'd be happy to hook up with if lightning strikes. You can load the dice.

So when I hear people defend gay rights by saying, "Of course it's not a choice, who would choose to be queer, who would choose to be oppressed and vilified and discriminated against?" My reaction is to raise my hand and say, "Me. Over here. I would." Of course I'd rather not be oppressed, etc.—but even with all of those drawbacks, I'd still choose to be queer. And I'd still choose to be in a queer relationship. I did.

Most Americans Know Someone Who Is Gay

Liberals are more likely than conservatives to know someone who
is gay, but majorities in both groups know at least one person who
identifies as gay or lesbian.

*Do you have any friends, relatives, or coworkers who have
told you personally that they are gay or lesbian?*

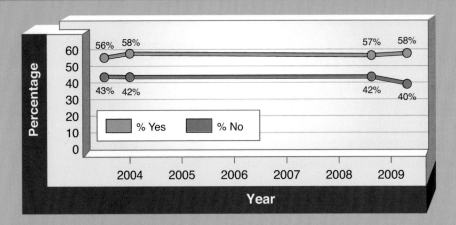

Do you personally know someone who is gay or lesbian?

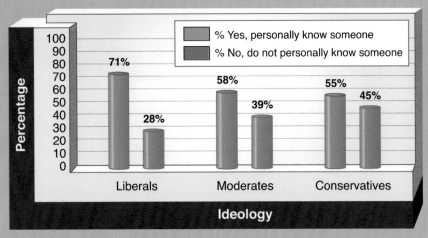

Examining personal experience by ideology, 71 percent of self-
identified liberals say they personally know someone who is gay or
lesbian—far more than is true among moderates and conservatives,
who align more closely with the national average.

Taken from: *USA TODAY*/Gallup Poll, May 7–10, 2009.

The author argues that gay people deserve rights whether or not they choose their sexual identity.

Choice Should Have Nothing to Do with Rights

And this is a big part of the reason that I think the "choice" issue is a red herring in the gay rights debates. After all, you could argue that pedophiles[1] don't choose to be attracted to children, and still think it's profoundly immoral to act on that attraction. The important question in the gay rights debates is not whether being queer is a choice, but whether there's any reason whatsoever to think that being queer is harmful. And by now, the evidence is overwhelming that it is not. Whether it's a choice or not is irrelevant. It is still, flatly and unequivocally, none of anybody else's damn business.

1. People who are sexually attracted to children.

EVALUATING THE AUTHOR'S ARGUMENTS:

Greta Christina argues that choice should have no bearing on rights. That is, in her opinion, people who choose to be Muslim should have no fewer rights than people who do not; likewise, people who are born to be killers, rapists, or child molesters should have no right to act on those impulses simply because they cannot help it. What do you think? Do you agree with her reasoning? If yes, explain why it makes sense. If not, explain why you think choice matters in the gay rights debate.

Viewpoint

4

Therapy Can Cure People of Homosexuality

Joseph Nicolosi, interviewed by David W. Virtue

"We believe that all people are heterosexual, but that some heterosexuals have a homosexual problem."

Joseph Nicolosi, who heads the National Association for Research & Therapy of Homosexuality, is a therapist who practices gay conversion therapy. He claims to help gay people renounce their sexuality and become straight. In this interview with David W. Virtue, who writes on the website VirtueOnline.org, Nicolosi argues that homosexuality is the result of childhood trauma. He believes that if people can get to the root of this trauma, they can be cured of their homosexuality. He recounts how he has helped gay people reduce their homosexual urges, fall in love with their opposite-sex spouse, and renounce their homosexuality completely. Homosexuality, he says, is a disorder that can be cured with therapy and practice.

AS YOU READ, CONSIDER THE FOLLOWING QUESTIONS:
1. What kind of early trauma does Nicolosi believe results in homosexuality?
2. What, according to the author, "strikes at the heart of the gay agenda"?
3. What does Nicolosi say is described as a gnat buzzing around one's ear?

*V*irtue Online: Is there a gay gene?

    Nicolosi: After 35 years of investigation, they still have not discovered the Gay gene. After 36 years since the APA [American Psychiatric Association] dropped its diagnosis of Homosexuality and during that period of time, no credible child developmental model has emerged, to explain the homosexual condition without traumatizing the child. In other words, that fact remains that if you traumatize a child in a particular way you will create a homosexual condition. If you do not traumatize a child, he will be heterosexual. If you do not traumatize a child in a particular way, he will be heterosexual. The nature of that trauma is an early attachment break during the bonding phase with the father. . . .

Is "once gay always gay" true?

    A central cornerstone of gay propaganda is "once gay always gay." It is amazing how the gay agenda has successfully convinced most people that one is either gay or straight, determined of course by the mythological gay gene.

    What is particularly shocking for me is that many church leaders actually believe that God created two kinds of people—homosexual and heterosexual. We believe that all people are heterosexual, but that some heterosexuals have a homosexual problem.

Is there a predisposition to homosexuality?

    We have been conceding the possibility of temperamental predisposition, usually described as timid, shy, non-aggressive, artistic and introverted. We can debate that assumption. Since as we believe the homosexual condition begins with an intense but insecure attachment to the mother, we attribute that to temperament. It may in fact be a consequence of a fragile attachment to a secure relationship with the mother.

    John Bowlby, the great pioneer in childhood attachment, described the child who had an insecure attachment to his mother as being timid shy, introverted and he wasn't even talking about homosexuality. It is from the insecure relationship with the mother that the boy is unprepared to bond with the typically distant detached emotionally aloof and/or hostile father.

A woman protests government support of conversion therapy for gays in China. However, because a biological explanation for homosexuality has not been proved, the author believes it is possible to convert gay people to heterosexuality.

What happened in 1973 when the APA said homosexuality was no longer a disordered behavior?

It is amazing to think in one day in 1973, 100 years of child studies in psychoanalytic literature was completely thrown out and homosexuality was pronounced "normal."

The three great pioneers of psychoanalysis, [Sigmund] Freud, [Carl] Jung and [Alfred] Adler all saw homosexuality as disordered and the entire development of psychoanalytic research continued until one day in 1973.

To paraphrase Oscar Wilde, "It is the gene that dare not speak its name." No one is supposed to ask causation. The consequence to our profession is an intimidating research environment in which clinicians and researchers can no longer explore causation of a condition that many find distressful.

Do men and women come to you voluntarily?
   Absolutely.

So where does the queer opposition's understanding come from and why do they hate the possibility of change, if someone voluntarily knocks on your door and says, "help me"?
   Supposedly, they are coming in because of their "unresolved internalized homophobia." The only acceptable treatment, therefore, must be not to give the client what he is asking for, but to give the client precisely what he is not asking for.

The justification for denying the client's autonomy and self-determination is the arrogant assumption that "we know better what's good for you than you do." We will tell you what your problem is, which is to learn to enjoy gay sex. So drop your inhibitions drop your archaic religious beliefs, forget your morality or ethic and join the gay parade.

Who are the "we"?
   The "we" is not science; the "we" are the gay activists who have a monopoly on public policies disseminated through the mental health associations.

There seems to be a coerciveness about the gay agenda, that it is no longer an issue of free choice.
   True. It is not even respecting human dignity. It is a violation of freedom of choice. The client seeking help to develop his heterosexual potential to diminish what he finds distressful in his life must be abandoned. His dream for a wife, marriage, children, white picket fence, and a traditional lifestyle must be discarded because gay activism knows better. They are happy being gay so you must be too.

You have said the Great Lie in homosexuality is "once gay always gay." Can you elaborate?

Central to the gay agenda and its determined goal to have complete homosexual acceptance as normal and natural, is the belief that certain people are just born gay. Gay activists are very familiar with many opinion surveys, which show consistently that if people believe gays are born that way and therefore have no choice, there will be greater tolerance and acceptance. But if you introduce the possibility of choice, then there is less tolerance. So every time a man stands up and says "I was once homosexual and am no longer," that strikes at the heart of the gay agenda.

I believe that the gay rights movement has gained sufficient success in popular acceptance and

> **FAST FACT**
>
> In 2009 the journal *BMC Psychiatry* reported that 4 percent of British psychiatrists and psychologists said they would be willing to help gay patients try to convert to heterosexuality, and 17 percent said they had tried to help patients reduce gay feelings at least once in their careers.

the acquisition of rights and civil liberties that they no longer need to feel threatened by ex-gay testimonies. I believe that the gay community is now sufficiently accepted by the popular culture that they can now afford to allow individuals to transition out of homosexuality without the need to disparage a former homosexual's life story.

In your practice over 25 years, what sort of success have you experienced and what about failure?

I can say that the most important determinant in therapeutic success is motivation. If the client is highly motivated, barring additional psychological problems, he will experience significant diminishment in his same sex attractions. There are individuals who experience no change, so success cannot be guaranteed for everyone, but I can tell you that over the past 25 years as a clinical director supervising seven therapists at a clinic which treats about 135 ongoing cases a week, we have developed our techniques and therapeutic interventions such that we can bring about greater change in a shorter period of time. All things being equal, we now expect the client to experience significant change in two or three months.

Are they cured?

This is not to say he or she is completely "cured" of homosexuality and the process may take many years, perhaps a lifetime, but he will acquire skills and self understanding to have his homosexual temptations become less and less until they become insignificant. One man described it as being finally and occasionally like a gnat buzzing around his ear.

Have you ever experienced clients who completely got over their homosexuality?

Absolutely. Yes. I am working with a 63 year old man who has been struggling with homosexuality all his life. Six months in therapy with me, he has no homosexual attractions and no homosexual temptations at all and he now is complaining that his life is boring because so much of his life was taken up with gay porn and gay fantasies. By the way, we did it all on SKYPE. He is based in Sydney, Australia.

What are the ratios of success?

I used to say one-third no change, one-third significant improvement and one-third treatment success. It is getting to be more are successfully shedding their unwanted same sex attractions. I see the numbers for complete improvement. For many who claim not to be completely "cured," it is less and less till it is little more than a gnat.

Tell me about the third that fail?

That third consists of teenagers dragged in by parents who don't want to be there. Husbands dragged in by their wives or individuals sent by their pastors and priests who don't want to be there. This returns us to motivation, which is essential.

Another segment of the homosexual population who may fail but who are motivated have additional psychological issues that impede their treatment success.

Such as?

Addictions, low impulse control, narcissistic personality disorder, inability to self reflect and clinical depression, to name some.

A well known American evangelical leader recently came out of the closet. You have undoubtedly read about him. He later said (within four months that he had been cured). What is your diagnosis of him?

Can Gay Conversion Therapy Work?

A seven-year study of 98 patients (72 men and 26 women) found that 23 percent of patients "converted" to heterosexuality after undergoing treatment. However, the American Psychiatric Association warns that such therapy has serious potential risks, including depression, anxiety, and self-destructive behavior.

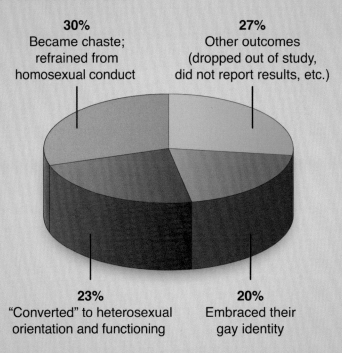

30%
Became chaste; refrained from homosexual conduct

27%
Other outcomes (dropped out of study, did not report results, etc.)

23%
"Converted" to heterosexual orientation and functioning

20%
Embraced their gay identity

Taken from: Stanton L. Jones and Mark A. Yarhouse, "A Longitudinal Study of Attempted Religiously–Mediated Sexual Orientation Change," *Journal of Sexual Marital Therapy*, vol. 37, 2011.

I would ask has he dealt with the underlying causes of his homosexuality. Uncompromising honesty with oneself is a necessary requirement to treatment success. If he has beaten it in four months, he should write a book about how he did it. It would be an instant bestseller. I would buy a copy.

You talk about a number of great myths about homosexuality. The first is that 10% of the population is gay. Is that true?

That was a lie promoted by Alfred Kinsey over 60 years ago and it has become the standard cry of gay activists and the standard claim of homosexual apologists. In fact, it is 1.5 percent to 2 percent. Kinsey himself had a personal interest in inflating the percentage because he himself was homosexual.

Once "gay always gay"?

Not true. There is no gay gene. It is a myth. The cry is that the homosexual is normal in every other way except for his sexual preference. Not true, it is the opposite. There are deep-seated personality differences, which create the condition and in fact, homosexuality is only the tip of the iceberg, a mere symptom of a deeper personality conflict.

Are you seeing more ex-gay people?

It is wonderful to see men and women in greater numbers standing up publicly and telling their story of overcoming unwanted same sex attractions. Ten years ago, we could not find one person who would go public. Today a young person struggling with such feelings can look to many models of individuals who preceded him. Today there are websites with numerous individuals telling their stories in front of a camera. At a recent concert in Italy, an Italian pop singer named Povia did a great song called "Luca was gay" introducing the ex-gay character into the pop culture. It was a touching moment. . . .

What does this portend for the future?

There is a great momentum building toward the recognition and respect for the man or woman desiring a heterosexual life.

EVALUATING THE AUTHOR'S ARGUMENTS:

In this viewpoint, Joseph Nicolosi describes the people he treats as "patients." In the following viewpoint, Wayne Besen describes them as "victims." Which do you think is a more accurate term for people who undergo gay conversion therapy? Why? Explain your reasoning using material drawn from the viewpoints.

Viewpoint

5

Gay Conversion Therapy Harms People and Is Homophobic

Wayne Besen

"These therapies don't make clients heterosexual. . . . All that is accomplished . . . is enticing vulnerable clients to pay dearly for the identical shame and repression they previously received for free."

In the following viewpoint, Wayne Besen argues that gay conversion therapy damages people, denies reality, and demonizes homosexuality. He argues that therapists who think they can convert gay people to heterosexuality misunderstand the nature of both sexuality and therapy. Undergoing gay conversion therapy does not help people become straight, argues Besen. Rather, it only makes them feel bad about themselves and more confused about their identity and how to express it in a healthy way. He concludes that it is unethical to suppress people's natural interests and identities and that gay conversion therapy is a sham that should be put to rest.

Besen is an author, activist, columnist, and public speaker. He runs the website Truth Wins Out, where this viewpoint was originally published.

AS YOU READ, CONSIDER THE FOLLOWING QUESTIONS:
1. How did Besen's parents react when he told them he was gay?
2. Who are John Paulk and Michael Johnston, and how do they factor into the author's argument?
3. Who, according to Besen, is constantly on the verge of tears?

By the time victims of so-called "ex-gay" or conversion therapy reach me at TruthWinsOut.org, their self-esteem has been trampled and their self-worth is non-existent. These individuals were often betrayed by therapists who were supposed to be helping, but turned out to be the root cause of their enormous pain and suffering.

Sadly, such therapists have aligned themselves with religious organizations that send the detrimental message that if a gay client refuses to undergo sexual conversion or commit to a lifetime of celibacy he or she will be socially ostracized or will burn in Hell. From my experience, I have yet to see how such coercive and cruel treatment is conducive to good mental health.

The "Ex-Gay" Movement Is a Scam

Having studied the "ex-gay" movement for a decade and authored a book on the topic, *Anything but Straight: Unmasking the Scandals and Lies Behind the "Ex-Gay" Myth*, I have found that conversion therapy is ineffective, harmful and anachronistic. These therapies don't make clients heterosexual, nor do they help reconcile faith and sexuality. All that is accomplished, unfortunately, is enticing vulnerable clients to pay dearly for the identical shame and repression they previously received for free.

Regrettably, a well-financed cottage industry has arisen to deny reality and distort the lives of gay and lesbian people. This is evidenced by a group of politically motivated right wing counselors who filed a formal complaint in February with the American Counseling Association [ACA] falsely claiming that the ACA had violated its own polices and had stigmatized the beliefs of Christian counselors. Its real goal, however, was to bully the ACA into allowing some practitioners to harm clients, while shielding this damage in the cloak of religious liberty.

In another example, last summer, right wing therapists wrote a letter to protest the American Psychological Association. They were expressing their outrage over an APA task force that will review current scientific research and stances on conversion therapy in a brazen attempt to intimidate the reviewers.

On behalf of the survivors of such therapy, I implore all mental health associations to withstand such political interference and resist the attempt to mainstream fringe therapies that harm gay and lesbian Americans.

There are three primary reasons why such therapy models should be definitively rejected. First, they confuse stereotypes with science. Secondly, they lack peer review studies and evidence that such therapies work—while there is a growing body of evidence that they hurt large numbers of people. Third, they rely on bizarre techniques that are a blight on the field of mental health.

Confusing Myths with Science

I came out to my parents as a gay man in 1988 at the age of eighteen. Their first reaction was shock and the second was to try to "fix" me. Shortly after my revelation, my mother and father presented me with an audiotape, "Gay and Unhappy" that claimed it could turn me straight. I listened intently to a deep hypnotic voice that spoke over New Age music that told me I liked breasts and the way women smelled.

When this desperate measure did not work, my parents found a book that claimed I could succeed at sexual conversion. I soon learned that my homosexuality supposedly came from a distant father and weak prowess at sports. The book also suggested that the elusive cure was having non-sexual relationships with same-sex peers. This was baffling to me because I was very close to my dad, was an all-city basketball player in high school and had many heterosexual male friends that I wasn't attracted to. According to the literature of conversion therapists, I should not have been gay.

Therapists, such as Dr. Joseph Nicolosi, president of the National Association for Research and Therapy of Homosexuality, further confuse myths with sound medicine. The doctor has repeatedly said at Focus on the Family seminars, "We advise fathers, if you don't hug your sons, some other man will." Nicolosi also encourages his male clients to drink Gatorade and call friends "dude" to increase their masculinity. Additionally, the doctor makes false statements about gay life, saying, "I do not believe that any man can ever be truly at peace in living out a homosexual orientation."

Homosexuality Is Normal and Common

On the twentieth anniversary of my coming out experience, legions of Americans have also chosen to live honestly and openly. We now have countless examples of gay men and lesbians who grew up in loving homes and excelled in sports. Indeed, there are even examples of former professional athletes who are gay, such as former pro baseball player Billy Bean and former pro football player Esera Tuaola.

Over the last two decades we have learned through empirical evidence that the simplistic cause and effect model offered by ex-gay therapists does not conform to reality. As the masses have come out, we now know that gay and lesbian people come from every imaginable background—just as straight Americans do. Any therapist that suggests otherwise clearly has not spoken to actual gay people and has not done the necessary research to make judgments on the etiology of homosexuality.

No Evidence That Therapy Is Safe or Effective

Ex-gay therapists lack peer review studies offering proof that their therapy is effective and not harmful to their clients. Their statistics are either inconsistent or non-existent. The only examples of "success" have come from non-peer-reviewed "research" at fundamentalist institutions that harshly condemn homosexuality and ban openly gay students—such as Pat Robertson's Regent University.

The most noted "research" supporting the ex-gay viewpoint was Dr. Robert Spitzer's controversial 2001 study that concluded a select few subjects highly motivated by religious belief could improve heterosexual functioning. This study made national news because in 1973 the Columbia University professor helped spearhead the removal of homosexuality as a mental disorder from the American Psychiatric Association's *Diagnostic and Statistical Manual* [*of Mental Disorders*].

However, the study' methodological flaws included using subjects who made their livings as anti-gay lobbyists. There was no accounting for bisexuality. The research did not include the vast majority of people who leave ex-gay programs dissatisfied. And, no physical tests were used to measure the veracity of his subjects' statements or their sexual attractions. Essentially, the study consisted of Spitzer periodically calling handpicked anti-gay lobbyists on the telephone and asking them if they had gone from gay to straight. This was the equivalent of calling up employees of Phillip Morris once a year to ask them if smoking had harmed them.

Furthermore, Dr. Spitzer has repeatedly chastised right wing political organizations for exploiting and exaggerating his work and has gone out of his way to say that change is extremely rare. For example, on May 28, 2006 he told the *Los Angeles Times*, "If some people can change—and I think they can—it's a pretty rare phenomenon."

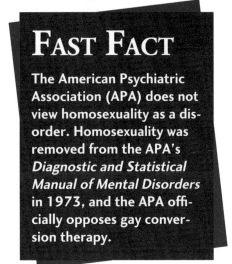

FAST FACT

The American Psychiatric Association (APA) does not view homosexuality as a disorder. Homosexuality was removed from the APA's *Diagnostic and Statistical Manual of Mental Disorders* in 1973, and the APA officially opposes gay conversion therapy.

It Is Unethical to Try to Change People

So, why is there a multi-million dollar industry devoted to "changing" people when the most optimistic study calls the possibility for a positive outcome a "pretty rare phenomenon"? Is it ethical to ruin the lives of thousands of gay people and their unsuspecting straight spouses for the remote possibility that one person might experience a small degree of change in their sexual orientation?

And, the possibility of any shift in attraction is highly suspect when one considers that most ex-gay testimonials come from paid staffers at political organizations, such as Exodus International or Focus on the Family. We rarely find independent people who claim long-term success that are not compensated political lobbyists—thus presenting a clear conflict of interest, since they derive their livelihood from their personal stories. In addition, even many of the high profile ex-gays who appear in the media have later come out of the closet or resigned in disgrace for not living as advertised.

People rally against gay marriage and in favor of other antigay programs, such as conversion therapy. Having undergone such therapy himself, the author argues that conversion therapy has no value.

For example, Focus on the Family' ex-gay leader, John Paulk, was photographed in a gay bar in 2001. In 2003, Rev. Jerry Falwell's ex-gay spokesperson, Michael Johnston, resigned after it was found he was having sexual relations with men he met on the Internet. The founder of Homosexuals Anonymous, Colin Cook, resigned after he was found to be having sex with his clients. The co-founder of Exodus International, Michael Bussee, left his wife and children to live with another male ex-gay minister. Indeed, the more the right wing tries to convince Americans that sexual conversion is possible, the more unlikely it seems.

Denying Reality and Demonizing Homosexuality

Ex-gay ministers and therapists also use questionable techniques, such as exorcisms to rid gay people of the "demon of homosexuality." They sometimes instruct clients to wear rubber bands on their wrists and snap them whenever they find a person physically attractive. Other times, "touch therapy" is employed, where the counselor caresses (sometimes abusively) a client sitting on his or her lap.

Equally damaging are religious counselors, such as Dr. Warren Throckmorton, who actually promote the peculiar notion that a person can effectively separate sexual identity from attraction. The idea that one can spend an entire lifetime in such obvious denial is usually untenable and often a recipe for inner-turmoil. Having extensively studied the ex-gay movement, it is my observation that this idea of the "happy celibate homosexual" is a mental health mirage. The people I have met at ex-gay conferences who are living in this state of love-limbo are hopelessly despondent and constantly on the verge of tears.

End the Torment

No one is suggesting that therapists alter their personal beliefs. However, religion cannot be used as a shield for practitioners who contribute to and exacerbate their clients' suffering. It is crucial to the integrity of all mental health associations that they soundly reject politically tainted attempts to mainstream fringe psychological practices that have caused so much misery and dysfunction.

Right wing psychologists should also be denied permission to create a parallel system under the auspices of religious freedom. All patients —regardless of the belief systems of their doctors—should be able to receive the highest standard of care derived from strict adherence to the latest science and rigorous ethical standards. Conversion therapy fails to meet this test and is a cause for much unnecessary torment— not a solution for those who are conflicted by their sexual orientation and religious beliefs.

EVALUATING THE AUTHOR'S ARGUMENTS:

To make his argument, Wayne Besen shares how his parents tried to suppress and deny his sexuality when he came out to them. Does knowing his background and his first-hand experience with this issue make you more or less likely to agree with his position? Why or why not?

Chapter 2

How Should Sexual Orientation Be Handled in Schools?

Students in Texas demonstrate for the right to form a gay-straight alliance club at their school. Gay clubs in schools have become a hot-button issue.

Gay Clubs Should Be Allowed in Schools

Aidan Johnson

> "Many gay teenagers harm themselves today out of shame. The last thing they need is a ban on clubs that offer them support."

Aidan Johnson is a lawyer. In the following viewpoint, he argues that schools should not ban gay clubs. He discusses events in Ontario, Canada, where state-funded Catholic schools have banned gay-straight alliance clubs, groups in which gay and straight students meet to discuss gay rights and support each other. He says such clubs are important for teens, many of whom are bullied and/or rejected by their churches or families, or who otherwise struggle with their identities. To ban such clubs is to perpetuate the shame and alienation of gay people, which Johnson says is both immoral and antithetical to Catholic beliefs. He concludes that gay clubs should be allowed in schools because they help teens find grounding during a difficult time in their lives.

1. As reported in the viewpoint, what is an "equality club" and how does it differ from a "gay-straight alliance club"?
2. Why, according to Johnson, were Catholic school rights initially written into the Canadian Constitution?
3. What does the phrase "amnesiac denial" mean in the context of the viewpoint?

The Charter of Rights[1] is many splendoured. But like all beautiful things, it contains paradoxes. As school resumes across Canada this month [September 2011], one Charter paradox in particular will weigh on many students' lives: the ban on gay-rights clubs enforced in Ontario's state-funded Catholic schools.

FAST FACT

A 2011 study published in the journal *Pediatrics* found that lesbian, gay, and bisexual students are five times more likely to attempt suicide than straight students, but those who went to schools with gay-straight alliances and antidiscrimination policies were significantly less likely to attempt suicide.

A Mean-Spirited Ban

Last November [2010], the Catholic school board in the Southern Ontario community of Halton passed a resolution banning "gay-straight alliances"— clubs in which gay and straight high-school students meet to talk about and promote gay rights. Other school boards then confirmed they have similar bans.

Gay students in the Catholic schools say their rights to free expression, assembly and equality give them the further right to form gay liberation clubs. The Catholic boards say their right to operate distinctly Catholic schools— guaranteed by the British North America Act and Section 29 of the Charter—allows them to block at least some gay equality projects on school grounds.

1. A document that guarantees various political and civil rights to Canadians.

As a compromise, the boards have said students can form broad-based "equity clubs." The clubs can promote homosexual and transgender equality alongside racial equality and rights for women and the disabled, but they can't use the word "gay" in the club name. Apparently, the key difference between an equity club and a gay-straight alliance is that an equity club promotes equality for all, while the alliance clubs are more narrowly focused. Also, the alliance clubs call themselves "gay."

The boards knew they were on thin ice banning discussion of homosexual rights entirely. The equity clubs are the answer—a way to avoid officially censoring the conversation, while keeping the word "gay" off the morning announcements. The Jesuit art of equivocation lives on.

Lost Lives

Antigay bullying led to a rash of suicides by gay teen boys in 2010 and 2011. Some studies have shown the presence of gay clubs on school campuses can help gay teens feel more supported and reduce antigay bullying.

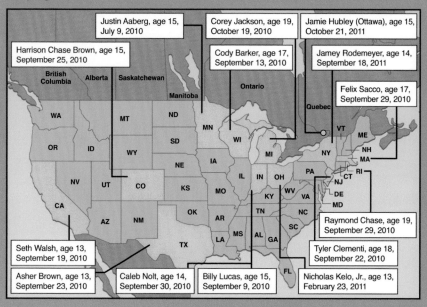

Justin Aaberg, age 15, July 9, 2010

Corey Jackson, age 19, October 19, 2010

Jamie Hubley (Ottawa), age 15, October 21, 2011

Harrison Chase Brown, age 15, September 25, 2010

Cody Barker, age 17, September 13, 2010

Jamey Rodemeyer, age 14, September 18, 2011

Felix Sacco, age 17, September 29, 2010

Raymond Chase, age 19, September 29, 2010

Seth Walsh, age 13, September 19, 2010

Tyler Clementi, age 18, September 22, 2010

Asher Brown, age 13, September 23, 2010

Caleb Nolt, age 14, September 30, 2010

Billy Lucas, age 15, September 9, 2010

Nicholas Kelo, Jr., age 13, February 23, 2011

Catholicism Should Promote and Protect Minorities

Ironically, the Fathers of Confederation wrote Catholic school rights into the Constitution because they wanted to protect minorities. Catholics were then a profoundly marginalized group, and many of their schools were francophone [French speaking]. Preserving them was a way of shielding what most French Canadians saw as an elemental part of their identity. Still other Catholic schools had large numbers of Irish, who also were intent on preserving their culture.

The Catholic schools were a way of making peace. In protecting them, the Constitution advanced its project of enshrining respect for diversity as a central value. Today, the ban on gay-rights clubs in Ontario's Catholic schools stands as an amnesiac denial of the Catholic education law's history and what that law means.

Many Catholics support gay rights. They defy their leaders and offer theological arguments for doing so. Unfortunately for gay students, these Catholics are not in charge of the Church. Nor, for the most part, are they in charge of the Catholic school boards.

Aaron Cryer, president of the gay-straight alliance club at a Portland, Oregon, high school, speaks at a school assembly about the need for gay clubs to help build discrimination-free school environments.

Do Not Shame Gay Teens

The debate over gay-rights clubs is part of a broader controversy in Canadian schools as to what should be taught about homosexuality in the classroom. Where does it leave many families' religious views, for instance, if students must learn about gay sex alongside straight sex in health class?

I am a gay man who grew up Catholic. My relationship with the Church is complicated. On one hand, I know that Catholicism is tied up with my sense of compassion and of Irish heritage. But I also know that the Church made me ashamed for a long time.

Many gay teenagers harm themselves today out of shame. The last thing they need is a ban on clubs that offer them support.

EVALUATING THE AUTHOR'S ARGUMENTS:

In this viewpoint, Aidan Johnson used examples, historical facts, and reasoning to make his argument that gay clubs should not be banned from schools. He did not, however, use any quotations to support his point. If you were to rewrite this article and insert quotations, from what authorities might you quote? Where would you place the quotes, and why?

Gay Clubs Should Not Be Allowed in Schools

Dennis Todd

"Schools are not the place for social experimentation or promotion of lifestyles that injure and kill many of its own members."

In the following viewpoint, Dennis Todd argues that gay clubs should not be allowed in schools. Gay clubs are not like chess clubs, he says—in his opinion, they promote an immoral and dangerous lifestyle that threatens impressionable children. He worries that gay clubs will confuse students, many of whom are at an impressionable and experimental point in their lives. Todd argues that homosexuals have higher rates of depression and disease, and thus schools should not support clubs that facilitate or glorify homosexuality. He concludes that gay clubs would threaten many more students than they would assist. In his view, school is not an appropriate place to promote controversial lifestyles like homosexuality.

Todd is a licensed school psychologist.

The ACLU [American Civil Liberties Union] intends to sue the Nassau County School District pressuring schools into allowing gay clubs equal access on campus. One of their legal positions rests on the notion that, other than sexual proclivity, homosexuals are no different than heterosexuals and therefore should enjoy the same club privileges as, say, chess enthusiasts. Leaving aside the principled absurdity of that position there are very serious moral, psychological and health consequences that we should be aware of if such clubs are allowed.

Do Not Force Schools to Promote a Risky Lifestyle

As a school psychologist in private practice I have counseled and worked with homosexual students, helping them deal with feelings and problems. I, and my professional organization, actively promote the rights of homosexual students to be treated equally and to be free from harassment. I agree with this policy as does every school administrator I've worked with over the past 30 years.

However the Gay-Straight Alliance seems to want our community to believe otherwise and turn the gay club issue into one of "free speech." It is much more than that because it involves public education's indirect approval of a destructive and deadly lifestyle, promoted to impressionable adolescents during a time when they themselves are experimenting and developing their personality and sexual identities. We should never subject our students to harm under the guise of freedom of expression. Restricting gay clubs in order to protect vulnerable kids from homosexual experimentation is no more a violation of free speech than it is to prohibit falsely yelling fire in a theater. Both are dangerous and require restrictions.

Gay-Straight Alliance Clubs in the United States

As of 2011, schools in seventeen states did not have a gay-straight alliance network, an organization that fights homophobia, bullying, and other campus issues.

States without a gay-straight alliance network

Taken from: Gay-straight alliance network, December 2011. www.gsanetwork.org.

The Truth About the Nature of Homosexuality

In 1973, the same year that the Supreme Court legalized abortions, the American Psychiatric Association removed homosexuality as a disorder from its diagnostic manual. Their reasoning was based primarily on genuine empathy and political pressure, but virtually no scientific data. They remarkably included a "conscience" criteria stating that homosexuality may only be considered a problem if an individual actually feels bad about it. Dr. Charles Socarides, an APA task force member, now admits that removing homosexuality as a diagnosis disregarded 70 years of research showing the grave risks of homosexual activity, including the emergence of an "addictive component."

Most studies now agree that the incidence of genetically determined homosexuality is lower than previously estimated, falling somewhere between 2–3 percent. The National Association for Research & Therapy of Homosexuality suggests that behavioral experiences (exposure, environment, etc.) may actually be more important in causing individuals to experiment with homosexual behavior, though they have no genetic predisposition for doing so. The researchers also found that poor father-son relationships and early exposure to homosexual experiences contributed greatly to later homosexuality. Enrique Rojas, a prominent psychiatrist, goes even further to suggest that the majority of homosexual orientation stems from environmental factors, not genetic.

It Is Wrong to Encourage Children to Be Gay

Experimentation is a well-known phenomenon in adolescent development. That's the real problem here. To promote homosexual behavior as a "gay" lifestyle is alarmingly deceptive to children. Kathleen Melonakos, a former nurse at Stanford University Medical Center, urges that homosexual lifestyles be more accurately described as a serious "pathological addiction." Promiscuity, anonymous rendezvous and bizarre sexual acts are common despite the lethal medical consequences associated with persisting in such behavior.

The list of medical problems is daunting and shows homosexual behavior to be more deadly than smoking, alcoholism or drug addiction. Melonakos saw no other group dying of infectious diseases in their mid-forties except practicing homosexuals, mainly

FAST FACT

As of 2012, about four thousand gay-straight alliances were registered with the Gay, Lesbian and Straight Education Network.

men. The Centers for Disease Control readily admits that homosexual men are a thousand times more likely to contract AIDS than the general heterosexual population.

Homosexual behavior presents destructive moral and social effects for children and families. It's not that homosexuality itself is bad or wrong; rather it's the promotion of homosexual behavior that can cause moral confusion and depression in developing adolescents. While students with a strong moral and family foundation may be

Many oppose the formation of gay clubs in schools, contending that such clubs are harmful to vulnerable adolescents.

immune to homosexual advocacy or indoctrination, others who are on the fringes of school social life can easily be drawn to gay clubs simply because they are accepted there.

Gay Clubs Hurt Children

Serious reflection on intended and unintended consequences of gay clubs on campus is essential. Here a few points to consider:

1. Adolescence is a period when meaning is found for sexual feelings, attractions, and behaviors. It is a key point in time when most children begin to form sexual identity. Heterosexual interactions and some sexual experimentation are typical at this age. While 2–3 percent of adolescents know or suspect they are homosexual, the remaining 97 percent are not, but may remain open to experimentation. Adolescence is marked by trials of risky behavior. Non-homosexual youth who engage in homosexual experimentation can result in identity confusion, depression and life-long psychological problems.

2. Homosexual behavior spreads disease. One study reports that the average homosexual has between 20 and 100 partners per year (average heterosexual has 8 partners in a lifetime). Although they make up only 2–3 percent of the population they account for 60 percent of all syphilis cases.

3. In another study, 73 percent of psychiatrists report that homosexuals are less happy than the general population and that their unhappiness is not due to social stigmatization.

4. The median age for homosexual deaths is 42 for males and 45 for females.

5. 33 percent of homosexuals admit to minor/adult sex. One in 20 homosexuals commit child molestations (opposed to 1 in 490 heterosexual molesters).

6. Adolescents who are mentally challenged, socially awkward or emotionally immature are quite vulnerable and can be drawn to cliques and factions outside the mainstream of traditional school culture.

7. The rights of Christian parents who do not want their children exposed to clubs promoting homosexual lifestyles are equally important yet their opportunity to promote Christian clubs is restricted.

8. While they may not openly admit it, gay students recruit members for a variety of psychological and social reasons. Off-campus clubs can just as effectively provide opportunities for advocating without offending Christians or risk harm to impressionable students.

Gay Clubs Are Different from Chess Clubs

In my practice I've never had an adolescent come to me for counseling because of losing a match in a chess club. But I've had non-homosexual adolescents come to me depressed because of a one-night homosexual stand and then had thoughts of killing themselves. I believe that gay clubs will increase these problems. The decision to allow them in our schools has more dangerous consequences for 97 percent of our heterosexual students than it has in benefits for the 3 percent who might be homosexual. In the final analysis, public schools are not the place for social experimentation or promotion of lifestyles that injure and kill many of its own members.

EVALUATING THE AUTHOR'S ARGUMENTS:

Dennis Todd and Aidan Johnson, who authored the previous viewpoint, disagree over whether gay clubs should be allowed in schools. After reading both viewpoints, what is your opinion on whether gay clubs should be allowed in schools? What pieces of evidence or arguments influenced you?

LGBT Issues Should Be Taught in Schools

San Francisco Chronicle

> "*The role of gays and lesbians also deserves fair treatment in lessons about the development of this state and nation.*"

In the following viewpoint, editors at the *San Francisco Chronicle* argue that gay history should be taught in schools. They explain that textbooks are continually revised to include groups of Americans who have been marginalized or otherwise left out of the American story. African Americans, Latinos, Asians, and women are among the groups that were initially ignored by textbooks; now, the histories, struggles, and contributions of such groups are a basic part of most curricula. So, too, should be the case with gay history, the editors argue. They conclude that not teaching gay history in schools compromises history and enshrines bigotry in the classroom.

AS YOU READ, CONSIDER THE FOLLOWING QUESTIONS:
1. What are at least five things that SB48, the bill that proposes teaching gay history, does *not* do, according to the authors?
2. What topics does Mark Leno say might be included in history books that have been updated to include gay history?
3. Who is Tom Ammiano, and how does he factor into the author's argument?

School textbooks evolve, just like the society the pages describe. The contributions of African Americans, Latinos, Asians and women—all missing or minimized in decades past—are now more fully and accurately portrayed in textbooks and other instructional materials. The role of gays and lesbians also deserves fair treatment in lessons about the development of this state and nation.

Let Us Include All Who Have Contributed to History

That's the simple and forceful premise behind a bill, SB48, now [July 10, 2011] on Gov. Jerry Brown's desk.[1] But the idea of highlighting gay people's contributions still draws controversy in a state where same-sex marriage remains illegal and a political wedge issue. In this case, the opposition is misguided about what's at stake.

The measure, authored by Sen. Mark Leno, a San Francisco Democrat, doesn't specify language, description or illustrations. It doesn't glorify or promulgate a "gay agenda," as opponents contend. It doesn't denigrate religion, call out long-dead historical figures or directly instruct small children on a delicate subject.

In fact, while much of the focus has been on the bill's call for the inclusion of gay and lesbian contributions to our history, it also adds religion and physical disability to the list of characteristics for which instructional materials must not "reflect adversely"—just as current law prohibits schools from making negative portrayals on the basis of race, gender or national origin.

> ## FAST FACT
>
> The Southern Poverty Law Center Reports that homosexuals are 2.4 times more likely to suffer a violent hate crime attack than Jews, 2.6 times more likely than blacks, 4.4 times more likely than Muslims, 13.8 times more likely than Latinos, and 41.5 times more likely than whites.

Adding a Missing Page

This is not about micromanaging or political correctness. School officials will retain wide latitude to implement the law. This is merely an

---

1. Brown signed the bill into law on July 14, 2011.

California state senators Christine Kehoe and Mark Leno embrace after passage of a highly controversial measure to require the teaching of gay history in California schools.

overdue requirement that schools not disparage people with stereotypes or ignore critical parts of our history.

"We are conspicuous in our absence in the curriculum," Leno said. "A page of civil rights is missing, and it's an important page—especially in California."

This deserved changeover is still incomplete without the recognition of the contributions of gays, lesbians, bisexuals and transgender

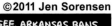

populations covered by the bill. These groups, who find no public acknowledgment in schoolbooks, are prone to suicide, depression and anti-gay hostility that thrives in the historical vacuum.

"I Don't Want to Be Invisible"

Should the governor sign the law, the next steps would be taken by the state school board, which would select new textbooks in 2016, a wait obliged by a depleted state budget. This panel and local school boards would have a voice in overseeing the classroom use and curriculum for the books. Local boards would also determine which age groups would get the new textbooks intended for social science courses. It's nothing like a one-size-fits-all dictate from Sacramento.

So what would the updated books read like? Leno, the bill's sponsor, imagined a fuller description of the gay rights movements of the last few decades, "beginning back with the view that homosexuality was a mental illness" to the efforts to allow gays and lesbians to marry and serve openly in the military.

"We've come light years," said Leno. "How do you overlook that?"

Added San Francisco Assemblyman Tom Ammiano, also a Democrat: "I don't want to be invisible in a textbook." Ammiano, who shepherded the measure through his chamber, said: "History that's omitted, revised or ignored just isn't history."

We Should Teach a Complete History

The textbook law moved through both sides of the Legislature on Democratic majorities. But that's happened before, when a similar bill was vetoed by Gov. Arnold Schwarzenegger in 2006.

Brown has a chance to correct the mistake. His signature would mandate that the existence and struggles of gay people be recorded in schoolbooks, not left out. It would be an important change that acknowledges an overlooked segment of society and also yields a truer history of this country.

EVALUATING THE AUTHOR'S ARGUMENTS:

Editors at the *San Francisco Chronicle* argue that gay, lesbian, bisexual, and transgendered people have contributed to the state of California and the nation and thus deserve a place in history textbooks. What is at least one counterargument put forth by the editors of the *Los Angeles Times* in the following viewpoint? Explain that argument, and then state the position with which you agree.

Viewpoint

4

LGBT Issues Should Not Be Taught in Schools

Los Angeles Times

"Politicians don't write good textbooks, and they shouldn't try."

Laws that would require textbooks to feature gay history are a bad idea, argue the editors of the *Los Angeles Times* in the following viewpoint. The editors agree that gay, lesbian, bisexual, and transgendered people have made important contributions to the nation, some of which have a legitimate place in the classroom. But they say that forcing textbooks to include their story will likely result in inaccuracies and bias. They also warn that textbooks are already crowded with so much information that it has become impossible to treat subjects in good detail. In their opinion, gay history should not be mandated. Textbooks should be written by historians and experts, not by politicians with a fleeting and pointed political agenda.

AS YOU READ, CONSIDER THE FOLLOWING QUESTIONS:
1. As described in the viewpoint, what happened in Texas when lawmakers mandated changes to state history books?
2. With what do the editors say teachers already struggle?
3. As reported in the viewpoint, how must the elderly and African AIDS victims be portrayed in textbooks, according to HB48?

Politicians don't write good textbooks, and they shouldn't try. That's true in Texas, where conservatives on the state Board of Education ordered up change in history books, such as minimizing the racism inherent in the interning of 100,000 Japanese Americans during World War II, downplaying the role of founding father Thomas Jefferson in part because he coined the phrase "separation of church and state," and reducing references to Islam.

Experts, Not Politicians, Should Write Curriculum

It's also true in California, where liberals in the Legislature are pushing a bill [SB48] that would require textbooks to include, according to *Times* reporter Patrick McGreevy, "the role and contributions of lesbian, gay, bisexual and transgender Americans." A similar bill was vetoed by then-Gov. Arnold Schwarzenegger in 2006.

A couple prepares to sign a petition to repeal state law SB48, which requires California schools to teach gay history. Many conservative and religious groups oppose the law.

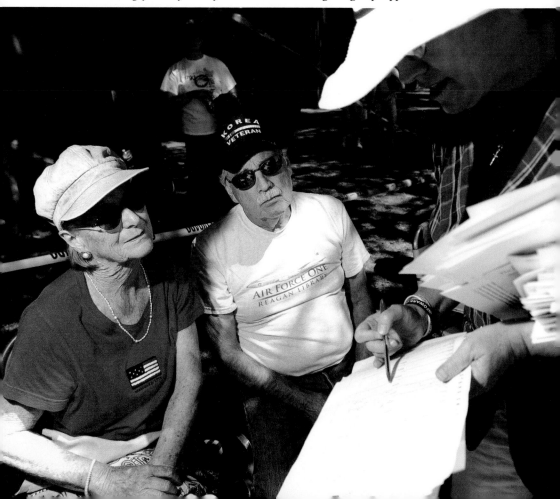

Americans Do Not Want LGBT Issues Taught in Elementary Schools

A May 2011 poll found the majority of Americans do not want gay history or gay lifestyle issues to become part of required school curricula.

Question: "Is it appropriate to expose elementary school students to 'gay pride' and 'Gay History Month' lessons that celebrate the lives of homosexual activists like Harvey Milk?"

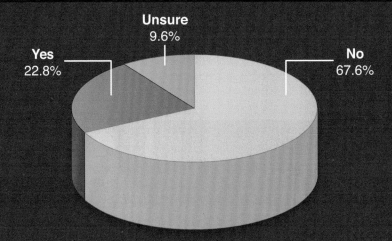

Unsure
9.6%

Yes
22.8%

No
67.6%

Question: "Do you believe elementary school children should be taught that homosexuality is a normal alternative lifestyle?"

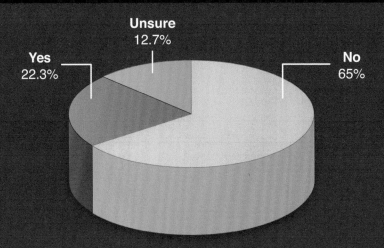

Unsure
12.7%

Yes
22.3%

No
65%

Taken from: *WorldNetDaily* and Wenzel Strategies, April 19–21, 2011.

Does the idea have a better chance five years later, with Jerry Brown as governor?[1] We hope not. Years ago, California made the wise decision to have experts draw up a balanced social studies curriculum that became a model for schools nationwide. Legislators aren't improving education in the state by stuffing the curriculum with new politically correct requirements, any more than Texas board members improved education there.

Textbooks Are Already Crowded

That's not to say textbooks shouldn't address the struggle against discrimination based on sexual orientation. Though there is still a long way to go, gays and lesbians have made huge gains in recent decades and are now making history with their quest for full marriage rights. These battles no doubt have a legitimate place in the social studies curriculum. But that's a decision for educators and textbook writers to make. If more is added to the social studies curriculum, something else will have to be deleted or treated more shallowly. Teachers already struggle to get through all the required material before the state's standardized tests are administered in the spring.

The bill, SB48, adds to an overly long list of requirements, some more reasonable than others, that have been pressed upon the state's textbooks over the years. Minority groups, the elderly and the disabled must be represented proportionally and never portrayed in a bad light. People in poor countries aren't supposed to be shown as poor, lest they be stereotyped, and information on AIDS in Africa must not reflect negatively on the continent. So poor people aren't poor and the elderly are physically fit and financially sound, according to the textbooks—and we complain that students are poorly educated.

> **FAST FACT**
>
> On July 14, 2011, California became the first state to require that schools include the contributions of lesbian, gay, bisexual, and transgender people in social studies curricula.

1. Brown signed the bill into law on July 14, 2011.

History Suffers When Driven by Politics

Fables don't make for solid instruction. History is the great story of people, groups and movements—their faults as well as their accomplishments—shaping the world up through the events of today. It is a story best told by historians, not by politicians.

Chapter 3

What Laws Should Be Made Regarding Sexual Orientation?

Hatred and violence against gays has led to the passage of laws that protect them by banning crimes of discrimination based on sexual orientation. Such laws are a point of heated controversy.

Viewpoint
1

The LGBT Community Needs More Legal Rights

Tracy Baim

"Some Americans 'like us, they really like us,' while others would fire us, take away our children, deny us the right to adopt or foster children, ban us from marrying, and, in some cases, kill us."

Tracy Baim is the publisher of the *Windy City Times*, a Chicago-based newspaper geared toward the LGBT community in that city. In the following viewpoint, she argues that Americans continue to hate, attack, and even kill gay people. Although some legal gains have been made, these have taken decades and come at the expense of people's jobs, families—even their lives. Gay youth suffer bullying so extreme that some turn to suicide; other gay Americans have been beaten to death by mobs. Antigay rhetoric is commonplace. Baim says it is difficult to feel that progress has been made when large swaths of the public continue to think homosexuals are sinful, wrong, or otherwise unworthy of rights. She concludes that the LGBT community needs more rights and greater protections, ones that are permanent and long lasting.

AS YOU READ, CONSIDER THE FOLLOWING QUESTIONS:
  1. Who is Marcellus Andrews and how does he factor into Baim's argument?
  2. Who is Matthew Shepard and how does he factor into Baim's argument?
  3. According to the author, what percentage of Americans think sexual relations between two same-sex adults is always wrong?

Despite decades of progress on LGBT rights, there continue to be bullying-related suicides among our youth, including 14-year-old Jamey Rodemeyer,[1] attacks on our people, including 19-year-old Marcellus Andrews,[2] of Waterloo, Iowa; and sports figures like hockey player Wayne Simmonds who just naturally spew anti-gay hate as a way to attack opponents.

Decades of Murder and Hate

These are "now" events, not "then." Skimming the pages of the gay press from the 1970s to the 1990s, there were many high-profile cases of harassment and murder, suicide and despair. Some of these made mainstream headlines, such as the murder of Charles Howard 27 years ago. Howard was thrown over a bridge into the Kenduskeag Stream in Bangor, Maine on July 7, 1984. Three boys pled guilty to the killing, which allowed them to serve minimal time, because they were teens (15, 16 and 17). Howard was 23 when he was killed, and his case sparked a national outrage.

> **FAST FACT**
>
> According to the National Center for Transgender Equality and the National Gay and Lesbian Task Force, 53 percent of transgendered Americans report being verbally harassed in a public space, including hotels, restaurants, buses, airports, and government agencies.

1. In September 2011 Rodemeyer killed himself after being victimized by bullies.
2. A gay teen who was beaten to death in Iowa in August 2011.

The vicious 1998 murder of Matthew Shepard painfully highlighted the violence perpetrated against members of the gay community.

Flash forward 14 years: in October 1998, Matthew Shepard, 21, was brutally murdered near Laramie, Wyo., causing more national outrage. Spurred by the then-nascent Internet, his crime took on international proportions and still is a basis for educating about hate and violence. There is now a federal hate-crimes statute named for Matthew and fellow hate victim James Byrd, and his family carries on his name through the Matthew Shepard Foundation, which has just announced a multi-million-dollar "American Giving Awards" contest.

Some Americans Would Oppress, Attack, and Kill Gays

Now, in 2011, we have seen major successes, such as the removal of DADT.[3] But this progress is overshadowed by continued harassment and even murder. So it's hard to get excited about a new report showing that Americans are moving "dramatically toward acceptance of homosexuality." Some Americans "like us, they really like us," while others would fire us, take away our children, deny us the right to adopt or foster children, ban us from marrying, and, in some cases, kill us.

3. Don't Ask, Don't Tell, the policy that prevented openly gay people from serving in the military. Its repeal in 2010 was effected in 2011.

This newest study, "Public Attitudes Toward Homosexuality," is by NORC at the University of Chicago, an independent research organization headquartered in downtown Chicago.

NORC reports: "In addition to a plurality who now approve of same-sex marriage, Americans overwhelmingly support basic civil liberties and freedom of expression for gays and lesbians, in contrast to sharp division on such issues in the 1970s." This shows a "trend toward greater tolerance regarding homosexuality," said Tom W. Smith, director of the General Social Survey (GSS) at NORC and author of the NORC report.

The Road to Acceptance Has Been Long, Hard, and Hateful

The rise in support for same-sex marriage went from 11 percent approval in 1988 to 46 percent in 2010, compared to 40 percent who were opposed, according to NORC, which based its findings of

© 2003 by Mike Lane and CagleCartoons.com.

the latest GSS, conducted in 2010 with a cross sample of more than 2,000 people. NORC added:

> In 2010, 26 percent of the people surveyed who were under 30 said they felt same-sex behavior is "always wrong," while 63 percent of the people aged 70 and older held that opinion. . . . Although 44 percent of the people surveyed felt that sexual relations between two adults of the same sex is always wrong, another 41 percent thought such relations were "not wrong at all."

And even more depressing to think about is that the following issues are even up for debate, according to NORC:

> Support for a gay person's right to speak before a public audience increased from 62 percent in 1972 to 86 percent in 2010; support for allowing gays and lesbians to teach at colleges or universities rose from 48 percent in 1973 to 84 percent in 2010; and approval for having a library keep a book that favors homosexuality rose from 54 percent in 1973 to 78 percent in 2010.

Equality Still Eludes Homosexuals

What bothers me most are the questions themselves. If you surveyed most Americans, many would probably think some Latinos, African Americans or even the president don't have some of those rights. We have to move away from a society that precariously hinges our rights on the whims of popular opinion. That path resulted in the ban on same-sex marriage in California and other states. And it is a path that will never lead to equality.

EVALUATING THE AUTHOR'S ARGUMENTS:

Tracy Baim notes that Americans increasingly support allowing gays to teach college classes, letting gays address audiences in public, and allowing libraries to house gay-friendly books. But she says what bothers her is "the questions themselves." What do you think she means by this? Explain her position in one or two paragraphs.

The LGBT Community Does Not Need More Legal Rights

Justin Raimondo

"Gays an oppressed minority group? I don't think so."

In the following viewpoint, Justin Raimondo argues that the members of the LGBT community already have the legal rights they need to live as equal citizens. What they seek, he claims, is social acceptance of their lifestyle. He says the early gay rights movement made important strides in outlawing bans on homosexual conduct. But more recent efforts—such as the attempt to legalize gay marriage—are less about acquiring new rights and more about securing symbols of social acceptance. For example, he says that marriage is a heterosexual institution in which gays want to participate so that their relationships are seen as legitimate. Furthermore, gays are no oppressed minority, says Raimondo: They are among the most likely Americans to attend college, have good jobs, and earn healthy salaries. He says the gay rights movement is confused about the difference between earning rights and earning respect. He concludes the gay rights movement is misguided in trying to use the state to legislate acceptance of its lifestyle.

Raimondo is the editorial director of the website Antiwar.com and author of *Reclaiming the American Right: The Lost Legacy of the Conservative Movement*.

AS YOU READ, CONSIDER THE FOLLOWING QUESTIONS:
1. Gay Americans are how many times more likely than heterosexuals to graduate from college, according to GayAgenda.com?
2. According to Raimondo, the modern gay rights movement is meant to garner support from whom?
3. What should "gay pride" really mean, according to the author?

The gay-rights movement took its cues from the civil rights movement, modeling its grievances on those advanced by the moderate wing led by Dr. Martin Luther King [Jr.] and crafting a legislative agenda borrowed from the NAACP [National Association for the Advancement of Colored People] and allied organizations: the passage of anti-discrimination laws—covering housing, employment, and public accommodations—at the local and national level. Efforts to institutionalize gay marriage have followed this course, with "equality" as the goal.

Gays Are No Oppressed Minority Group

But the civil rights paradigm never really fit: unlike most African Americans, lesbians and gay men can render their minority status invisible. Furthermore, their economic status is not analogous— indeed, there are studies that show gay men, at least, are economically better off on average than heterosexuals. They tend to be better educated, have better jobs, and these days are not at all what one could call an oppressed minority. According to GayAgenda.com, "studies show that [gay] Americans are twice as likely to have graduated from college, twice as likely to have an individual income over $60,000 and twice as likely to have a household income of $250,000 or more."

Gays an oppressed minority group? I don't think so.

A Reasonable Start

The gay-liberation movement started as a protest against state oppression. The earliest gay-rights organizations, such as the Mattachine Society and the Daughters of Bilitis, sought to legalize homosexual activity, then illegal per se. The movement was radicalized in the 1960s over police harassment. A gay bar on New York City's Christopher Street, known as the Stonewall, was the scene of a three-day riot provoked by a police raid. Tired of being subjected to continual assault by the boys in blue, gay people fought back—and won. At the time, gay bars were under general attack from the New York State Liquor Authority, which pulled licenses as soon as a bar's reputation as a gay gathering place became apparent. Activists of that era concentrated their fire on the issues that really mattered to the gay person in the street: the legalization of homosexual conduct and the protection of gay institutions.

As gay activists grew older, however, and began to channel their political energy into the Democratic Party, they entered a new and more "moderate" phase. Instead of celebrating their unique identity and history, they undertook the arid quest for equality—which meant, in practice, battling "discrimination" in employment and housing, a marginal issue for most gay people—and finally taking up the crusade for gay marriage.

> # FAST FACT
>
> The Gay and Lesbian Service Organization reports that gay, lesbian, and bisexual Americans are twice as likely as the average American to have graduated from college, twice as likely to have an individual income over $60,000, and twice as likely to have a household income of $250,000 or more.

An Irrelevant Gay Rights Movement

Instead of battling the state, they began to use the state against their perceived enemies. As it became fashionable and politically correct to be "pro-gay," a propaganda campaign was undertaken in the public schools, epitomized by the infamous "Rainbow Curriculum" and the equally notorious tome for tots *Heather Has Two Mommies*. For

Opponents of gay rights contend that the legal rights already accorded to gays are sufficient. Demands for additional rights by the gay community, they say, are actually about gaining social acceptance of their lifestyle.

liberals, who see the state not as [German philosopher Friedrich] Nietzsche's "cold monster" but as a warm and caring therapist who is there to help, this was only natural. The Therapeutic State, after all, is meant to transform society into a liberal Utopia where no one judges anyone and everyone listens to NPR [National Public Radio].

These legislative efforts are largely educational: once enacted, anti-discrimination ordinances in housing, for example, are meant to show that the state is taking a side and indirectly teaching citizens a lesson—that it's wrong to discriminate against gays. The reality on the ground, however, is a different matter: since there's no way to know if one is being discriminated against on account of one's presumed sexuality—and since gays have the choice not to divulge that information—it is impossible to be sure if such discrimination has occurred, short of a "No Gays Need Apply" sign on the door. Moreover, landlords, even the bigots among them, are hardly upset when a couple of gays move in, fix up the place to look like something out of *House & Garden* [magazine], and pay the rent on time. The homosexual agenda of today has little relevance to the way gay people actually live their lives.

Gays Want Social Acceptance—They Already Have Rights

But the legislative agenda of the modern gay-rights movement is not meant to be useful to the gay person in the street: it is meant to garner support from heterosexual liberals and others with access to power. It is meant to assure the careers of aspiring gay politicos and boost the fortunes of the left wing of the Democratic Party. The gay-marriage campaign is the culmination of this distancing trend, the *reductio ad absurdum* [reducing to absurdity] of the civil rights paradigm.

The modern gay-rights movement is all about securing the symbols of societal acceptance. It is a defensive strategy, one that attempts to define homosexuals as an officially sanctioned victim group afflicted with an inherent disability, a disadvantage that must be compensated for legislatively. But if "gay pride" means anything, it means not wanting, needing, or seeking any sort of acceptance but self-acceptance. Marriage is a social institution designed by heterosexuals for heterosexuals: why should gay people settle for their cast-off hand-me-downs?

EVALUATING THE AUTHOR'S ARGUMENTS:

In the previous viewpoint, Tracy Baim describes members of the gay community as under threat of being fired, harassed, attacked, and even killed. In this viewpoint, Justin Raimondo describes a gay community made up of members who are highly educated and well paid and who seek broad acceptance of their lifestyle. In your opinion, which author's vision of the gay community is more accurate? Why?

Viewpoint

3

Gay Marriages Should Be Legal

"Denying gay men and lesbians the opportunity to marry because of their sexual orientation is essentially denying such individuals a basic human right."

Tyger Latham

Tyger Latham is a clinical psychologist who specializes in counseling gay patients and couples. In the following viewpoint, he explains why he thinks gay marriage should be legal. He cites studies that show gay couples are not significantly different from straight couples—people in both kinds of relationships are deeply attached to their partners and structure their lives around that commitment. Latham also points out that gay couples need the financial advantages that come with marriage and also deserve the psychological peace and stability that marriage offers. Latham argues that it is ridiculous to claim that same-sex marriages will undermine society. More married couples contribute to a stronger, healthier society, in his opinion. For all of these reasons he says that gay marriage should be legalized.

AS YOU READ, CONSIDER THE FOLLOWING QUESTIONS:

1. As reported in the viewpoint, how many states legalized same-sex marriage prior to New York's doing so in 2011?
2. What prominent psychological group endorsed same-sex marriage in 2004, according to the author?
3. According to Latham, do gay couples differ from straight couples in the satisfaction they derive from their relationships?

Yesterday, [July 24, 2011] hundreds of gay and lesbian couples across New York state wedded, marking a milestone for advocates for same-sex marriage. New York becomes the sixth and largest state to legalize gay marriage.

Gay Couples Are Much Like Straight Couples

Same-sex marriage remains a controversial issue, often eliciting strong emotions for those on both sides of the issue. Several years ago [in 2004], the American Psychological Association (APA) joined the debate and issued a public statement endorsing same-sex marriage. In presenting their position, the American Psychological Association cited a large and ever growing body of empirical research illustrating the harmful psychological effects of policies restricting marriage rights to same-sex couples.

> ## FAST FACT
>
> A 2011 poll taken by ABC News and the *Washington Post* found that 53 percent of Americans think gay marriage should be legal; 44 percent think it should be illegal.

Studies have shown that gay couples do not have significantly different relationships from those of heterosexual couples.

Americans Increasingly Support Same-Sex Marriage

In 2011, for the first time, more Americans supported legal same-sex marriage than opposed it.

Question: "Do you think it should be legal or illegal for gay and lesbian couples to get married?"

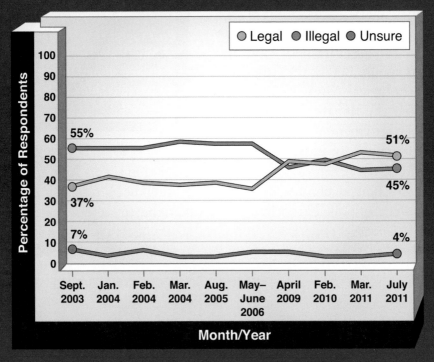

Taken from: ABC News/*Washington Post* poll, July 14–17, 2011.

Last year I spent some time reading and carefully examining the empirical research cited by APA. What the research says is that same-sex relationships closely resemble that of heterosexual partnerships. Like straight couples, gay and lesbian couples form deep emotional attachments and commitments. Furthermore, such couples do not fundamentally differ from heterosexual couples in their satisfaction with their relationships. The research suggests that there is no scientific reason to discriminate against lesbian and gay couples.

Marriage Is a Basic Human Right

Psychologists and other social scientists have long understood that marriage is an institution that profoundly affects the lives of those individuals who are allowed to participate in it. In addition to the significant financial advantages that come with marriage, the institution has important implications for the psychological and physical health of those who partake. Denying gay men and lesbians the opportunity to marry because of their sexual orientation is essentially denying such individuals a basic human right, including the psychological, physical, and financial opportunities that derive from that right.

Gay Marriage Strengthens Society

Critics of same-sex marriage have often emphasized the importance of "family values," and they are right to do so, as such values do exist and have significant consequences for society. For this reason (as well as others), the government has a responsibility to ensure that such values are protected. The strength of marriages is not just a function of physical attraction and procreation but also of external forces that serve as barriers, or perhaps constraints on dissolving the relationship. I think the critics are misguided in their fears that allowing gays and lesbians to marry will somehow erode the fabric of society and throw us into social chaos. In fact, the research suggests quite the opposite. Granting same-sex couples the right to marry is likely to lead to stronger and more psychologically and physically healthier families, something we should all be invested in protecting.

EVALUATING THE AUTHOR'S ARGUMENTS:

Because Tyger Latham is a psychologist, he approaches the issue of same-sex marriage from the perspective of psychological health. That is, he argues that legal same-sex marriage promotes psychologically healthy families, while denying same-sex marriage hurts gay couples' mental health. What kind of approach does Peter Sprigg, author of the following viewpoint, take? After reading both viewpoints, state the perspective with which you agree, and why.

Gay Marriages Should Not Be Legal

"*Legalization of same-sex marriage would utterly transform the meaning of the social institution, from one that exists primarily to ensure the birth and well-being of children into one primarily to gratify the desires of adults.*"

Peter Sprigg

In the following viewpoint, Peter Sprigg argues that gay marriage should not be legal. In his view, marriage is not about equality, nor is it about justifying the desires and decisions of adults. Primarily and historically, he says, marriage has been about children: creating them, raising them, and nurturing them. Same-sex couples cannot create children biologically, and thus the institution of marriage does not apply to them. He acknowledges that some same-sex couples might come to raise children—either as the result of divorce, adoption, artificial insemination, or other means. But Sprigg says marriage should not be changed to accommodate, or celebrate, these rare and unconventional cases. He believes marriage exists to provide children with mothers and fathers. Since same-sex couples can never provide this, he says there is no need to legalize their unions.

Sprigg is a senior fellow for policy studies at the Family Research Council, a conservative public policy and research organization.

D o children matter in Maryland?
    That is the question that will be at stake in 2011, when the Maryland legislature considers radically changing the definition of our most fundamental social institution—marriage.

Marriage Is About Children, Not Equality

The question of whether Maryland should place its highest stamp of official government affirmation on sexual unions between two men or two women actually has little to do with debates over "sexual orientation" and even less to do with bromides about "equality."

Opponents of gay marriage believe that the primary role of marriage is to produce children and that since same-sex couples cannot do so, the institution of marriage should not be available to them.

Instead, the core issue is whether the birth and nurture of children remains a priority in this state. It is the core issue because these have always been the central purposes of the social institution called marriage.

Some same-sex couples argue that they want to marry for the same reasons that many opposite-sex couples do. But the personal reasons why any one individual couple chooses to marry are also not the primary concern of the state.

Instead, the fundamental issue in debating the definition of marriage must be: What is the public purpose of marriage? Why is marriage treated as a public institution at all?

The Purpose of Marriage Is Reproduction

The answer was obvious to anyone who lived in any culture or civilization, anywhere in the world, throughout most of human history. Only in the present young century have some people become confused about it.

FAST FACT

According to the National Conference of State Legislatures, as of 2012 just six states—Massachusetts, Connecticut, Iowa, Vermont, New Hampshire, and New York—issued marriage licenses to same-sex couples (along with the District of Columbia).

Marriage is a public institution because it serves two public purposes: bringing together men and women for the reproduction of the human race and keeping together a man and woman to raise to maturity the children produced by their union.

The existence of future generations of children is fundamental to the survival of any society. The quality of their nurture is directly related to the quality of life in that society. Bonding the man and woman whose sexual union produces a child to one another and to that child is by far the most efficient way of ensuring that nurture.

Advocates of same-sex marriage claim that this concept (dubbed "responsible procreation" in several court decisions) cannot be the purpose of marriage because some opposite-sex couples marry without procreating. But again, this confuses the private purposes for marrying (which are not the legislature's business) with the public purposes of the institution of marriage (which are).

Opposite-sex relationships are the only type capable of producing children through natural intercourse and the only ones assured of providing children with both a mother and a father. Affirming only opposite-sex relationships as "marriage" thus makes perfect sense. But affirming same-sex relationships as "marriages" makes no sense. These relationships are incapable of producing children through their sexual union.

A Child's Birthright

And while some homosexual couples do raise children (most of whom were conceived in previous heterosexual relationships), such arrangements by definition deprive a child of his or her birthright to be raised by both a biological mother and father. Maryland may choose to tolerate and even protect such unconventional childrearing by allowing

Same-Sex Marriage in the United States

As of 2012, same-sex couples could marry in just a handful of states.

States with legal same-sex marriage

Taken from: Joan Schwartz, "After New York, New Look at Defense of Marriage Act," *New York Times*, June 27, 2011.

adoption by homosexual partners or couples. But it has no obligation to actively affirm and celebrate (through "marriage") the deliberate creation of permanently motherless or fatherless families.

The common-sense understanding that children should have both a mother and a father is now supported by reams of social science data. The research leaves no doubt that children raised by their own biological mother and father, who are committed to one another in a lifelong marriage, are happier, healthier and more prosperous than children in any other living situation. A recent (December 2010) study from the National Center for Health Statistics has reinforced this, demonstrating that children raised in the traditional "nuclear" family are less deprived in nine key areas of mental, physical and economic health. (Advocates of same-sex marriage counter this by pointing to supposedly favorable studies on homosexual parenting—but this handful of small, biased and methodologically unsound articles cannot refute the overwhelming findings on the importance of the natural mother-father family for children.)

Do Not Gratify Adults' Desires at the Expense of Children

Legalization of same-sex marriage would utterly transform the meaning of the social institution, from one that exists primarily to ensure the birth and well-being of children into one primarily to gratify the desires of adults.

Does Maryland need children? Do children need a mom and a dad?

The answer to both questions is: "Yes."

But if the legislature legalizes same-sex marriage, it would be declaring that the answer to both is "No."

This would be both a foolish and tragic choice.

> **EVALUATING THE AUTHOR'S ARGUMENTS:**
>
> Peter Sprigg argues it does not matter why men and women marry—only that their union produces children and that they stay together to raise them. Do you agree with Sprigg that this is the purpose of marriage? Why or why not?

Viewpoint

5

The Military Should Let Soldiers Be Open About Their Sexual Orientation

"At the end of the day, being gay does not render a soldier inadequate or unfit for duty."

Alex Peterson

Gay and lesbian soldiers should not have to hide their sexuality to serve their country, argues Alex Peterson in the following viewpoint. He applauds the repeal of Don't Ask, Don't Tell, a policy that prevented soldiers from disclosing their sexual orientation. Peterson says sexuality has nothing to do with how good a soldier someone is. Gay soldiers are unlikely to let their sexuality distract them while on duty, he says, and they can shoot guns just as well as straight people can. Peterson says the only requirements for military service should be a person's skills and fitness: Whom people love or how they conduct themselves in private has no bearing on their ability to be soldiers. He concludes that letting soldiers be honest about their sexual orientation results in a stronger military and a better country.

Alex Peterson, "Don't Ask, Don't Tell Repeal Necessary," *Point Park Globe* (Pittsburgh, PA), September 26, 2011. www.pointparkglobe.com. Copyright © 2011 by Point Park Globe. All rights reserved. Reproduced by permission.

Peterson is a gay soldier whose articles have appeared in the *Globe*, an independent newspaper of Point Park University in Pittsburgh, Pennsylvania.

AS YOU READ, CONSIDER THE FOLLOWING QUESTIONS:
1. What directive did President Ronald Reagan issue in 1982, according to Peterson?
2. What are gay men and women not any more likely to do than their straight counterparts, according to the author?
3. Why does the author think religious arguments against homosexuality are invalid?

D ating back to the Truman Administration in 1950, the act of discharging homosexual service members because of their sexual orientation has finally ended. The conclusion of such an undignified policy not only leaves our military and nation better off, but also provides for a much-needed recognition of equality amongst the gay community. However, as thrilled, happy, ecstatic and overjoyed as I am that Don't Ask Don't Tell (DADT) has finally been disbarred, I can't help but wonder: what was the big deal?

The History of Gays in the Military
DADT has a storied past, penned from the irreverent hands of several popular presidents. President Harry Truman's Uniform Code of Military Justice laid the groundwork for the legal discharge of openly gay servicemen and women in 1950. President Ronald Reagan then issued a defense directive in 1982 claiming, "homosexuality is incompatible with military service" and called for the dismissal of any service member who engaged in homosexual acts or stated their sexual preference. Finally, in an attempt to compromise after his election to office, President Bill Clinton introduced the most recent form of DADT after campaigning on the promise to lift the ban. So much for promises.

Despite the countless filibusters, stalling tactics and/or blockades issued by opponents of its repeal, Congress repealed DADT in December 2010, passing it along to President [Barack] Obama who signed the repeal into law on Dec. 22, 2010 and set a formal ending date [for DADT] of Sept. 20, 2011. Now that the history lesson is over, let's get to the real meat and potatoes of why I am writing this.

Why Are People So Scared of Gays?

Throughout my life, I've known many members of the military spanning the various branches: my father was a Marine, my aunt and uncle were both in the Air Force and my grandfather was an Army photographer. I don't claim to be an expert on the operation of a militia, nor do I know how to command a platoon of soldiers. With that being said, does a gay soldier really have that much impact on the success of our men and women in uniform? How does one soldier's sexual identity deviate from military compatibleness as President Reagan so aptly described? Also, why is the topic of homosexuality within the military so taboo? What are people so afraid of when it comes to the homosexual lifestyle?

I'm not expecting answers to these questions because any response worthy of my attention will never be offered. For me, DADT represented

President Barack Obama signs the repeal of Don't Ask, Don't Tell into law on December 22, 2010, making it legal for gays to serve openly in the US military.

all that is wrong with society. Gay soldiers were urged to deny who they were in order to protect the very nation who demanded their anonymity.

"Come, fight for us . . . but don't tell us you're gay."

"Here, take this gun, but please, if anyone asks, you're straight."

Homosexuality Is Perfectly Compatible with Military Service

I guess I just want to understand the purpose of such a despicable law. Gay men and women are not anymore likely to "hit on" members of the same sex any more than a straight person would pursue their respective mate. Just because a gay man bunks with a straight soldier doesn't automatically mean there will be an attraction. If you're a straight guy reading this, have you liked and pursued every girl you encountered? The answer is no, you haven't. Now, apply that concept to a gay soldier and you wind up realizing there isn't anything to be afraid of. Let's be honest: requiring gays to refrain from revealing their true selves only sheds light on the insecurities present in the commanding minds. How is that food for thought?

The repeal of DADT took too long. For 17 years, gays and lesbians were required to remain neutral on their sexual preferences, all the while ignoring who they really were. Lace up the boots of a gay soldier for a moment and imagine being 20 hours from home in a tent with fellow comrades speaking freely of their partners back home. I, as a gay soldier, however, can't. I can't tell them how much I miss my boyfriend or how long it has been since we last spoke in person. I can't share memories of when we would be together or even reveal that we have a sexual relationship. I can't love my partner here. Here, he's an absolution I'll never attest. Such a depiction paints the horror and pure insanity of the restrictions enforced by DADT.

> ## FAST FACT
>
> According to the Servicemembers Legal Defense Network, more than 14,500 gay and lesbian service members were discharged from the military under the Don't Ask, Don't Tell policy, which was repealed in 2011.

In 2010 Congress repealed Don't Ask, Don't Tell, which required soldiers to keep their sexuality secret. When the new policy of letting gay soldiers serve openly went into effect in September 2011, 68 percent of Americans expressed approval, while just 22 percent did not.

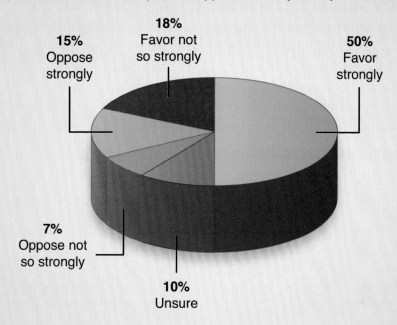

15%
Oppose
strongly

18%
Favor not
so strongly

50%
Favor
strongly

7%
Oppose not
so strongly

10%
Unsure

Taken from: CBS News Poll, September 28 through October 2, 2011.

Seeking Equality Is Not an "Agenda"

I don't believe that calling for the repeal of DADT caters to the "gay agenda," either. I have a question first though; what is the gay agenda anyway? If wanting equality and enjoying the same rights as heterosexuals constitutes having an agenda, then yes, I've got an agenda, but other than that, I'm stumped.

I'd like the opponents of the gay "agenda" out there to delve deep into their own identities and personalize a similar restriction on themselves. If you have been divorced, oops, sorry you can't serve in the military. If you have ever been publicly drunk or engaged in infidelity, you might want to stop filling out that recruitment form. If you like the color blue or enjoy women of a younger age, sorry I heard Giant Eagle is hiring. My point in all of that was to communicate that no one should be punished for who they are, good or bad (save for criminals). If you are willing to defend our country, your life outside of service should not hinder your performance on the front line or threaten your presence.

No One Should Be Punished for Who They Are

Being gay is not an option one makes, nor should it be the defining trait of a soldier willing to serve. I hold great respect for President Obama for his promise of killing DADT and following through on his word in a politically timely manner. At the end of the day, being gay does not render a soldier inadequate or unfit for duty. I want the advocates of DADT to reevaluate their prejudices, stereotypes and preconceived notions surrounding the gay community. It's not up to the Bible to determine who I love or to provide guidelines on how to live; therefore, religious arguments citing the blasphemy of homosexuality hold not an ounce of validity in debate.

At the risk of sounding cliché or pandering to the overused, our society must overcome differences and accept people however they wish to be. No one is asking for the befriending of every difference. What is reasonable to ask for, however, is the demonstration of civility toward someone who is simply different from you.

EVALUATING THE AUTHOR'S ARGUMENTS:

To make his argument, Alex Peterson discusses "the gay agenda." What does the gay agenda mean to him? What does it mean to Mackubin Thomas Owens, author of the following viewpoint? After considering the ways these two authors interpret the gay agenda, write one or two paragraphs on whether you think the gay agenda is real, threatening, or even important. Use evidence from the texts you have read to back up your answer.

The Military Should Not Let Soldiers Be Open About Their Sexual Orientation

Mackubin Thomas Owens

"Military readiness and effectiveness are to be subordinated to a political agenda. The United States military will be weakened as a result."

In the following viewpoint, Mackubin Thomas Owens argues that letting gay soldiers serve openly will weaken the US military. He argues that the military is for winning wars, not for conducting social experiments or granting civil rights. In his opinion, the Don't Ask, Don't Tell (DADT) policy, which prevented soldiers from disclosing their sexual orientation, struck a good balance. It preserved military functionality without infringing on gay soldiers' rights. DADT was repealed just a few weeks after Owens wrote this piece, and he warns that including openly gay soldiers will negatively affect unit cohesion and military readiness. He concludes that openly gay soldiers threaten the military's functionality and thus the safety of the entire nation.

Owens was in the Marine Corps during the Vietnam War. He is the editor of *Orbis*, a journal published by the Foreign Policy Research Institute, and the author of the book *US Civil-Military Relations After 9/11: Renegotiating the Civil-Military Bargain*.

AS YOU READ, CONSIDER THE FOLLOWING QUESTIONS:

1. According to Owens, what percentage of army troops said that serving with openly gay soldiers would negatively impact unit effectiveness? What percentage of marines had this opinion?
2. Why was the ban on openly gay soldiers different from the ban on African American soldiers, according to Owens?
3. As reported by the author, how many people were discharged from the military for homosexuality between 2004 and 2008? How many for drugs?

L ong before the Pentagon's report on the expected effects of repealing the current law prohibiting open homosexuals from serving in the U.S. military was released [in 2010], the conventional "narrative" had already been established thanks to leaks by anonymous individuals "familiar with the report's conclusions." That narrative holds that repeal of the current law would create "few risks" for military readiness, retention, and recruiting.

Soldiers Want Sexuality to Stay Secret

The conventional narrative makes much of the claim that most of the service members surveyed believe that repeal would not have a negative impact on military effectiveness. The key to "overcoming resistance" to repeal of the current law, the report concludes, is "training and education." Well, stand by for politically correct "sensitivity training" run amok. And the Marines and the Army will get it in spades because as the report shows, those services, the mission of which is to conduct close ground combat, are the most "resistant" of all.

Indeed, the report reveals that 45 percent of Army troops and nearly 60 percent of Marines (67 percent of those in Marine combat arms: infantry, artillery, and armor) who have been in combat zones say that repeal would have a negative impact on unit effectiveness. And this is the crux of the problem with the Pentagon report: it misses the point.

The Military's Job Is to Win Wars, Not Grant Civil Rights

The "functional imperative," i.e. the purpose of the U.S. armed forces is to fight and win the nation's wars. Success in combat requires trust and personal/unit bonding. But as a number of commentators have noted, the report does not identify a single benefit of repealing the ban when it comes to recruiting, retention, unit effectiveness, and readiness of the force.

Instead, the report seems to be predicated on the idea that the integration of open homosexuals into the military is merely the most recent manifestation of the quest for civil rights that began with African Americans after World War II. According to this view, lifting the ban against military service by open homosexuals is analogous to President [Harry] Truman's executive order racially integrating the military services.

Opponents of letting gays serve openly in the military warn it will weaken military readiness and erode unit cohesion.

But Truman's order was motivated by concerns about military effectiveness, not civil rights. For a variety of reasons, segregated African American units generally did not perform well on the battlefields of World War II. Truman's actions were in response to military-manpower experts who believed that integration would improve the military effectiveness of black soldiers.

The report repeatedly asserts that the actual difficulties of repealing the law will be less than the survey's responses would indicate. This is where "training and education," aka political correctness and sensitivity training, comes in.

Don't Ask, Don't Tell Worked Fine

The fact is that homosexuals serve honorably in the military. That was the purpose of the "don't ask, don't tell" policy compromise adopted by the Clinton administration after Congress passed the current law prohibiting service by open homosexuals. As a result of this policy, homosexuals who are willing to subordinate their "sexual orientation" to their duty are allowed for the most part to serve without interference.

> **FAST FACT**
>
> In 2010 the Department of Defense asked service members with combat experience how working with an openly gay soldier would affect their immediate unit's effectiveness at completing its mission. The majority—44.3 percent—said "negatively" or "very negatively."

The claim often found in the *New York Times* and the *Washington Post* that homosexuals are the victims of "witch hunts" is without merit. From 2004 until 2008, discharges for homosexuality averaged one third of one percent of all discharges. For instance, in 2008, there were 5,627 involuntary discharges for drugs, 3,817 for serious offenses, 4,555 for failure to meet weight standards, 2,353 for pregnancy, 2,574 for parenthood, and 634 for homosexuality, most of which resulted from voluntary statements, not "outing" by others.

The Pentagon report notwithstanding, the current arrangement seems to work quite well. So why the push to repeal the law and reverse

Countries That Allow Military Service by Openly Gay People

As of early 2012, twenty-six countries, shown here in gold, allowed gay people to serve openly in their militaries.

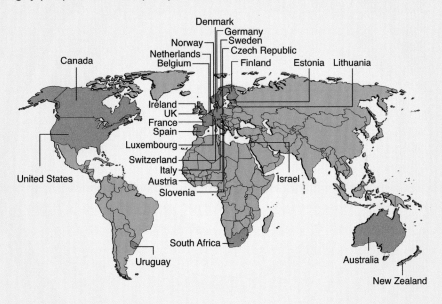

Taken from: Palm Center, www.palmcenter.org, 2011.

the "don't ask, don't tell" policy compromise? The short answer seems to be that this is not about individual homosexuals serving in the military but about a broader homosexual agenda.

The Reality of Gay Soldiers

What will the likely consequences of institutionalizing this political agenda be? The report doesn't sufficiently address them but a Marine colonel with substantial command time did so in an e-mail circulated some months ago.

What, he asks, does "serving openly as a homosexual" mean? Is all homosexual conduct permitted, e.g. cross dressing when going to the PX [store on a military base]? What conduct is *not* permitted?

Will "hate speech" policies apply to the armed forces after the repeal of the law? If a service member uses a term offensive to homosexuals, can he be charged with hate speech? Will commanders be required to take judicial action? If no judicial action is taken, will commanders be subject to civil or criminal suit by various homosexual political groups and their elected sponsors?

Will the personal opinion on homosexuality of a service member become an impediment to promotion or assignment to key billets? Are there any assignments to which homosexuals must be or may not be assigned?

Will the Senate and the House Armed Services committees demand sexuality statistics to make certain that homosexuals are being promoted at the same rate as non-homosexuals? Will homosexuals be promoted at a faster rate to "compensate" for previous years of discrimination?

What benefits will same-sex "partners" receive? How long must one have a relationship to qualify as a partner? Will partners of homosexuals be assigned to on-base housing? Do former partners of active duty homosexuals retain dependent benefits (like a divorced spouse) when divorce is not a legal option?

Will homosexual service members be permitted to date each other? Live with each other as partners in bachelor officer quarters (BOQ) or bachelor enlisted quarters (BEQ)? How does this affect fraternization regulations?

Will homosexuals be deployed to countries where homosexuality is a crime? If not, who picks up the slack?

A Weakened US Military

Such questions need to be addressed, but the Pentagon report largely ignores them. More importantly it ignores the impact of the issues raised by such questions on the effectiveness and readiness of U.S. forces and the consequences for retention and recruiting.

The Pentagon report is right to note that implementing repeal of the law can be done, but at what cost to U.S. security? The report makes it clear that military readiness and effectiveness are to be subordinated to a political agenda. The United States military will be weakened as a result.

Mackubin Thomas Owens claims that letting openly gay
soldiers serve in the military would interfere with the
trust and bonding that soldiers need to experience in
order to make military units effective. How do you think
Alex Peterson, author of the previous viewpoint, would
respond to this claim? After considering both viewpoints,
with which author do you ultimately agree, and why?

Facts About Sexual Orientation

Editor's note: These facts can be used in reports or papers to reinforce or add credibility when making important points or claims.

Facts About Sexual Orientation in America

According to an April 2011 report released by the Williams Institute at the University of California School of Law:

- More than 8 million American adults identify as lesbian, gay, or bisexual.
- Lesbian, gay, or bisexual adults make up 3.5 percent of the adult population.
- There are nearly seven hundred thousand transgender individuals in the United States—about 0.3 percent of the population.
- Together, about 9 million Americans—about the population of the state of New Jersey—identify as lesbian, gay, bisexual and transgendered (LGBT).
- Among adults who identify as lesbian, gay, or bisexual, a slight majority is made up of bisexuals (1.8 percent compared to 1.7 percent who identify as lesbian or gay).
- Women are substantially more likely than men to identify as bisexual.
- An estimated 19 million Americans (8.2 percent) report that they have engaged in same-sex sexual behavior.
- Nearly 25.6 million Americans (11 percent) acknowledge at least some same-sex sexual attraction.

In 2011 the Centers for Disease Control and Prevention published a comprehensive report on sexual identity in the United States. Among its findings:

- Twice as many women (13 percent) as men (5.2 percent) report having had any same-sex sexual contact in their lifetimes.
- Women with bachelor's degrees or higher were less likely to report same-sex sexual behavior than women in the other education categories.

- Men showed no significant differences by educational attainment.
- Hispanic women (6.3 percent) were less likely than either non-Hispanic white (15 percent) or non-Hispanic black (11 percent) women to report same-sex sexual behavior.
- Among men, non-Hispanic white men were more likely than either Hispanic men or non-Hispanic black men to report such behavior.
- Same-sex sexual behavior was reported by nearly 2 percent of boys and 10 percent of girls aged fifteen to seventeen.
- Women who reported four or more opposite-sex partners in their lifetimes were more likely to report any same-sex experience (20 percent) than those with fewer or none.

According to the Gay and Lesbian Alliance Against Defamation (GLAAD), gay characters make up 3.9 percent of scripted network television characters.

American Opinions About Sexual Orientation
A 2007 poll by CNN found the following about beliefs and attitudes toward homosexuality:
- 56 percent think sexual orientation cannot be changed;
- 42 percent think homosexuality results from upbringing and environment;
- 39 percent think homosexuality is something a person is born with.
- 57 percent said gay and lesbian couples should have the legal right to adopt children;
- 40 percent said they should not;
- 3 percent were unsure whether gay and lesbian couples should have this right.

According to a 2011 Quinnipiac University poll:
- 46 percent of Americans support a law that would allow same-sex couples to marry;
- 48 percent oppose such a law;
- 6 percent are unsure whether they support such a law.
- 44 percent of Americans think states that prohibit same-sex marriage should refuse to recognize legal same-sex marriages performed in other states;

- 49 percent think states should recognize legal same-sex marriages performed in other states;
- 7 percent are unsure whether states should recognize legal same-sex marriages performed in other states.
- 59 percent of Americans think same-sex marriage partners should be eligible for federal benefits;
- 35 percent think same-sex marriage partners should be denied federal benefits;
- 6 percent are unsure whether same-sex marriage partners should be eligible for federal benefits.

In 2011 the Public Religion Research Institute found the following:
- 65 percent of Americans believe places of worship contribute to higher rates of suicide among gay and lesbian youth.
- 72 percent said places of worship contribute to negative views of gay and lesbian people.
- 44 percent of Americans view same-sex relations as sinful.

A 2008 poll by the Gallup Organization found:
- Americans viewed homosexuality as less moral than divorce, gambling, the death penalty, embryonic stem cell research, heterosexual sex outside of marriage, medical testing on animals, having a baby outside of marriage, wearing clothing made of fur, and doctor-assisted suicide.
- Americans viewed homosexuality as more moral than abortion, suicide, cloning animals, cloning humans, polygamy, and having an affair.

A 2010 poll by the Gallup Organization found:
- 42 percent of Americans think homosexuality is morally acceptable;
- 43 percent of Americans think homosexuality is morally wrong.
- 53 percent of men think homosexuality is morally acceptable;
- 52 percent of women think homosexuality is morally acceptable.
- 62 percent of men aged eighteen to forty-nine think homosexuality is morally acceptable;
- 59 percent of women aged eighteen to forty-nine think homosexuality is morally acceptable.

- 44 percent of men fifty years and older think homosexuality is morally acceptable;
- 43 percent of women fifty years and older think homosexuality is morally acceptable.
- 35 percent of Republicans think homosexuality is morally acceptable;
- 61 percent of Democrats think homosexuality is morally acceptable;
- 61 percent of independents think homosexuality is morally acceptable.
- 33 percent of conservatives think homosexuality is morally acceptable;
- 64 percent of moderates think homosexuality is morally acceptable;
- 78 percent of liberals think homosexuality is morally acceptable.
- 42 percent of Protestants think homosexuality is morally acceptable;
- 62 percent of Catholics think homosexuality is morally acceptable;
- 85 percent of nonreligious people think homosexuality is morally acceptable;
- 84 percent of other non-Christians think homosexuality is morally acceptable.

Organizations to Contact

The editors have compiled the following list of organizations concerned with the issues debated in this book. The descriptions are derived from materials provided by the organizations. All have publications or information available for interested readers. The list was compiled on the date of publication of the present volume; the information provided here may change. Be aware that many organizations take several weeks or longer to respond to inquiries, so allow as much time as possible for the receipt of requested materials.

Advocates for Youth
2000 M St. NW, Ste. 750
Washington, DC 20036
(202) 419-3420
website: www.advocatesforyouth.org

Established in 1980 as the Center for Population Options, Advocates for Youth champions efforts to help young people make informed and responsible decisions about their reproductive and sexual health. The site offers a wealth of information about sexual orientation, homophobia, and antigay bullying.

American Civil Liberties Union (ACLU)
132 W. Forty-Third St.
New York, NY 10036
(212) 944-9800
website: www.aclu.org

The ACLU is the nation's oldest and largest civil liberties organization. Its Lesbian and Gay Rights/AIDS Project, started in 1986, handles litigation, education, and public policy work on behalf of gays and lesbians.

Children of Lesbians and Gays Everywhere (COLAGE)
1550 Bryant St., Ste. 830
San Francisco, CA 94103

(415) 861-5437
e-mail: colage@colage.org
website: www.colage.org

COLAGE provides support and advocacy for daughters and sons of lesbian, gay, bisexual, and transgender parents. Its website contains numerous reports, pamphlets, and other forms of information.

Family Equity Council
PO Box 206
Boston, MA 02133
website: www.familyequality.org

This organization works at all level of government to advance equality on behalf of LGBT families. Its mission is to strengthen communities, change hearts and minds, and advance social justice for all families.

Family Research Council (FRC)
801 G St. NW
Washington, DC 20001
(800) 225-4008
website: www.frc.org

The council is a research, resource, and educational organization that promotes the traditional family, which it defines as a group of people bound by marriage, blood, or adoption. It opposes gay marriage and adoption rights and publishes numerous reports from a conservative perspective on issues affecting the family, including homosexuality and same-sex marriage.

Family Research Institute (FRI)
PO Box 62640
Colorado Springs, CO 80962-0640
(303) 681-3113
website: www.familyresearchinst.org

The FRI distributes information about family, sexuality, and substance abuse issues. It opposes letting gays and lesbians serve openly in the military, legalizing gay marriage, and other issues. The institute publishes the bimonthly newsletter *Family Research Report* as well numerous position papers and opinion articles.

Focus on the Family
Colorado Springs, CO 80995
(800) 232-6459
website: www.family.org

Focus on the Family is a conservative Christian organization that promotes traditional family values and gender roles. Its publications include the monthly magazine *Focus on the Family* and numerous antigay marriage reports and articles.

Gay and Lesbian Alliance Against Defamation (GLAAD)
5455 Wilshire Blvd., #1500
Los Angeles, CA 90036
(323) 933-2240
website: www.glaad.org

This organization is dedicated to promoting and ensuring fair, accurate, and inclusive representation of individuals and events in all media as a means of eliminating homophobia and discrimination based on gender identity and sexual orientation. GLAAD works with news, entertainment, and social media to bring culture-changing stories of LGBT people into millions of homes and workplaces every day.

Gay, Lesbian and Straight Education Network (GLSEN)
90 Broad St., 2nd Fl.
New York, NY 10004
(212) 727-0135
e-mail: glsen@glsen.org
website: www.glsen.org

This organization strives to assure that each member of every school community is valued and respected regardless of sexual orientation or gender identity/expression. GLSEN seeks to develop school climates where difference is valued for the positive contribution it makes in creating a more vibrant and diverse community.

Lambda Legal Defense and Education Fund
120 Wall St., 19th Fl.
New York, NY 10005
(212) 995-8585
website: www.lambdalegal.org

Lambda is a public interest law firm committed to achieving full recognition of the civil rights of homosexuals. The firm addresses a variety of areas, including equal marriage rights, the military, parenting and relationship issues, and domestic partner benefits. It publishes the quarterly *Lambda Update* and the pamphlet *Freedom to Marry*.

National Center for Lesbian Rights
870 Market St., Ste. 570
San Francisco, CA 94102
(415) 392-6257
website: www.nclrights.org

The center is a public interest law office that provides legal counseling and representation for victims of sexual orientation discrimination. Primary areas of advice include child custody and parenting, employment, housing, the military, and insurance. The group's website has a useful "case docket" feature that keeps tabs on the outcomes of court cases related to gay and lesbian rights.

National Gay and Lesbian Task Force (NGLTF)
1325 Massachusetts Ave. NW, Ste. 600
Washington, DC 20005
(202) 393-5177
website: www.thetaskforce.org

The NGLTF is a civil rights advocacy organization that lobbies Congress and the White House on a range of civil rights issues. The organization works to make same-sex marriage legal. It publishes numerous papers and pamphlets, the booklet *To Have and to Hold: Organizing for Our Right to Marry*, and the fact sheet "Lesbian and Gay Families."

National Organization for Marriage
2029 K St. NW, Ste. 300
Washington, DC 20006
(609) 688-0450
e-mail: contact@nationformarriage.org
website: www.nationformarriage.org

This organization's mission is to protect marriage and the religious communities that sustain it. It was founded in 2007 in response to the growing movement to legalize same-sex marriage in state legislatures.

It publishes numerous fact sheets, reports, and other articles on why same-sex marriage should not be legalized.

Parents, Families and Friends of Lesbians and Gays (PFLAG)
1828 L St. NW, Ste. 660
Washington, DC 20036
e-mail: info@pflag.org
website: http://community.pflag.org

PFLAG is a national nonprofit organization with over 200,000 members and supporters and over 350 affiliates in the United States. This vast grassroots network offers support and information to parents, families, and friends of gay and lesbian Americans. The website offers some resources specific to schools and teachers.

Servicemembers Legal Defense Network (SLDN)
PO Box 65301
Washington, DC 20035-5301
(202) 328-3244 or (202) 328-3247
e-mail: sldn@sldn.org
website: www.sldn.org

The SLDN is a nonprofit legal services watchdog and policy organization dedicated to ending discrimination against and harassment of military personnel affected by Don't Ask, Don't Tell [DADT]. It works to end DADT, to ensure parity for LGBT service members, and to provide free, confidential legal services to all those impacted by DADT and related discrimination. Since 1993 its in-house legal team has responded to more than ten thousand requests for assistance.

**Sexuality Information and Education Council
of the United States (SIECUS)**
1012 Fourteenth St. NW, Ste. 107
Washington, DC 20005
(202) 265-2405
e-mail: mrodriguez@siecus.org
website: www.siecus.org

This national organization promotes comprehensive education about sexuality and advocates the right of individuals to make responsible sexual choices. Its website contains numerous fact sheets about the group's political action and advocacy efforts.

Traditional Values Coalition
139 C St. SE
Washington, DC 20003
(202) 547-8570
website: www.traditionalvalues.org

The coalition strives to restore what the group believes are traditional moral and spiritual values in American government, schools, media, and the fiber of American society. It believes that gay rights threaten the family unit and extend civil rights beyond what the coalition considers appropriate limits. The coalition publishes the quarterly newsletter *Traditional Values Report* as well as various information papers.

For Further Reading

Books

Ball, Carlos A., and Michael Bronski. *From the Closet to the Courtroom: Five LGBT Rights Lawsuits That Have Changed Our Nation*. Boston: Beacon, 2011. Offers analysis of five lawsuits that have been critical of the gay rights movement, including *Nabozny v. Podlesny* (1996), a gay bullying case, and *Romer v. Evans*, a sexual harassment case.

Boylan, Jennifer Finney. *I'm Looking Through You: Growing Up Haunted*. New York: Broadway, 2008. A rich, funny, and poignant memoir about a person named Jim who became Jennifer.

Corvino, John, and Maggie Gallagher. *Debating Same-Sex Marriage*. New York: Oxford University Press, 2012. Two opposing experts on gay marriage—one a philosopher and gay rights advocate, the other cofounder of the National Organization for Marriage and gay marriage opponent—debate critical questions about gay marriage, including what marriage is for, what effect legalized marriage would have on families and children, and whether legalized same-sex marriage will lead to polygamy.

Estes, Steve. *Ask and Tell: Gay and Lesbian Veterans Speak Out*. Chapel Hill: University of North Carolina Press, 2008. Draws on more than fifty interviews with gay and lesbian veterans to trace the evolution and history of the military's policy on homosexuality over a sixty-five-year period.

Savage, Dan, and Terry Miller. *It Gets Better: Coming Out, Overcoming Bullying, and Creating a Life Worth Living*. New York: Dutton, 2011. The creators of the It Gets Better project present a collection of essays from celebrities, everyday people, and teens who share their stories about overcoming bullying and getting to a place in life worth living.

Seefried, Josh. *Our Time: Breaking the Silence of "Don't Ask, Don't Tell."* New York: Penguin, 2011. Active-duty lesbian, gay, bisexual, and transgendered soldiers share their stories of serving under "Don't Ask, Don't Tell," revealing an intimate portrait of military life.

Periodicals and Internet Sources

Bauer, Gary. "Moonbeam Brings Queer Studies to California Grade Schools," *Washington Times*, August 3, 2011. www.washington times.com/news/2011/aug/3/moonbeam-brings-queer-studies-to -california-grade.

Bennett, Jessica. "Should Tyler Clementi's Bully Be Charged with a Hate Crime?," DailyBeast.com, April 22, 2011. www.thedaily beast.com/articles/2011/04/22/tyler-clementi-should-the-gay -teens-bully-be-charged-with-a-hate-crime.html.

Blankenhorn, David. "Protecting Marriage to Protect Children," *Los Angeles Times*, September 19, 2008. www.latimes.com/news /opinion/commentary/la-oe-blankenhorn19-2008sepl9.0.605 7126.story.

Boies, David. "Gay Marriage and the Constitution," *Wall Street Journal*, July 20, 2009. http://online.wsj.com/article/SB1248045 15860263587.html.

Boylan, Jennifer Finney. "We Want Cake, Too," *New York Times*, August 12, 2011. www.nytimes.com/2011/08/12/opinion/we-want -cake-too.html.

Center for American Progress. *All Children Matter: How Legal and Social Inequalities Hurt LGBT Families*, October 2011. www.family equality.org/site/DocServer/AllChildrenMatterFullFinal10212011 .pdf?docID=2401.

Chapman, Steve. "The Case for Gay Adoption," *Reason*, June 24, 2010. http://reason.com/archives/2008/12/01/the-case-for-gay-adoption.

Chrisler, Jennifer. "Why Gay Parents Are Good Parents," CNN .com, June 24, 2010. http://articles.cnn.com/2010-06-24/opinion /chrisler.gay.parents_1_adoptions-by-gay-people-anti-gay-gay -pride?_s=PM:OPINION.

Cushman, Candi. "Parents Beware: 'Anti-bullying' Initiatives Are Gay Activists' Latest Tools of Choice for Sneaking Homosexuality Lessons into Classrooms," CitizenLink, June/July 2010. http://fota .cdnetworks.net/truetolerance/p9_June_Jul_Citizen_10_anti bullying.pdf.

Cushman, Candi. "All Kids Should Be Protected from Bullying," *Huffington Post*, September 10, 2010. www.huffingtonpost.com /candi-cushman/all-kids-should-be-protec_b_712328.html.

Dejesus, Ivey. "'Gay-Conversion Therapy' Was Constantly Undermining My Sense of Self,' Central Pa. Man Says," *Harrisburg (PA) Patriot News*, August 27, 2011. www.pennlive.com/midstate/index.ssf/2011/08/gay-conversion_therapy_was_con.html.

Durkin, Tish. "Tyler Clementi and the Case Against 'Hate Crimes,'" *Week*, October 12, 2010. http://theweek.com/bullpen/column/208078/tyler-clementi-and-the-case-against-hate-crimes.

Grollman, Eric Anthony. "So What If Sexual Orientation Is a Choice After All?," National Sexuality Resource Center, San Francisco State University, January 25, 2010. http://nsrc.sfsu.edu/dialogues/users/grollman/blog/so-what-if-sexual-orientation-is-choice-after-all.

Honda, Mike. "Our Country Is Finally on the Path to Full Equality," *San Jose (CA) Mercury News*, August 4, 2011. www.mercurynews.com/sunnyvale/ci_18620391.

Kane, Gregory. "Dumb College Prank Gone Wrong Isn't a Hate Crime," *Washington (DC) Examiner*, October 6, 2010. http://washingtonexaminer.com/node/520457.

Kendall, Ryan. "Reparative Therapy Survivor Says Bachmann's Rhetoric Matters," *Advocate*, July 19, 2011. www.advocate.com/Politics/Commentary/OP-ED_Reparative_Therapy_Survivor_Says_Bachmann.

McEwen, Bill. "Gay Citizens Have Contributed to Our History," *Fresno (CA) Bee*, July 19, 2011. www.mcclatchydc.com/2011/07/19/v- print/117768/commentary-gay-citizens-have-contributed.html.

New York Times. "Gay People Around the World Face Bias, Abuse and Violence, a Study Reports," December 15, 2011. www.nytimes.com/2011/12/16/world/gay-people-around-the-world-face-bias-abuse-and-violence-a-study-reports.html?src=recg.

Perkins, Tony. "Christian Compassion Requires the Truth About Harms of Homosexuality," *Washington Post*, October 11, 2010. http://onfaith.washingtonpost.com/onfaith/guestvoices/2010/10/Christian_compassion_requires_the_truth_about_harms_of_homosexuality.html.

Pike, Deirdre. "Back-to-School Is Not Much Fun for Some," *Hamilton (ON) Spectator*, August 27, 2011.

Potok, Mark. "Anti-gay Hate Crimes: Doing the Math," *Intelligence Report*, no. 140, Winter 2010, Southern Poverty Law Center. www.splcenter.org/get-informed/intelligence-report/browse-all-issues/2010/winter/anti-gay-hate-crimes-doing-the-math.

Potok, Mark. "Gays Remain Minority Most Targeted by Hate Crimes," *Intelligence Report*, no. 140, Winter 2010. Southern Poverty Law Center. www.splcenter.org/get-informed/intelligence-report/browse-all-issues/2010/winter/under-attack-gays-remain-minority-mos.

Olsen, Theodore B. "The Conservative Case for Gay Marriage," Daily Beast.com, January 8, 2010. www.thedailybeast.com/newsweek/2010/01/08/the-conservative-case-for-gay-marriage.html.

Nardi, Peter M. "Conversion Therapy Fails to 'Pray Away the Gay,'" *Seattle Pacific Standard*, September 30, 2011. www.psmag.com/culture/conversion-therapy-fails-to-pray-away-the-gay-36569.

North, Oliver. "Gays in the Military," *National Review*, December 7, 2010. www.nationalreview.com/articles/254643/gays-military-oliver-north.

Reagan, Michael. "History Books Get Gay Makeover," GOP USA, July 7, 2011. www.gopusa.com/commentary/2011/07/07/reagan-history-books-get-gay-makeover.

Somerville, Margaret. "The Case Against Same-Sex Marriage," MercatorNet, July 28, 2011. www.mercatornet.com/articles/view/the case against same-sex_marriage.

Strudwick, Patrick. "The Ex-Gay Files: The Bizarre World of Gay-to-Straight Conversion," *Independent* (UK), February 10, 2010. www.independent.co.uk/news/uk/this-britain/the-exgay-files-the-bizarre-world-of-gaytostraight-conversion-1884947.html.

Strudwick, Patrick. "Conversion Therapy: She Tried to Make Me 'Pray Away the Gay,'" *Guardian* (Manchester, UK), May 26, 2011. www.guardian.co.uk/world/2011/may/27/gay-conversion-therapy-patrick-strudwick.

Sullivan, Andrew. "Why Gay Marriage Is Good for America," *Newsweek*, July 17, 2011. www.thedailybeast.com/newsweek/2011/07/17/andrew-sullivan-why-gay-marriage-is-good-for-america.html.

Toronto (ON) Globe and Mail. "End of the Rainbow," September 3, 2011.

Walker, Sirdeaner. "School Bullying Is Killing Our Children," *Black Press of America*, April 10, 2010. www.blackpressusa.com /op-ed/speaker.asp?NewsID=21485.

Whittemore, Katharine. "Making the Case for Gay Marriage," *Boston Globe*, June 24, 2011. http://articles.boston.com/2011-07-24/ae /29810429_1_gay-marriage-gay-couples-grant-marriage-licenses.

Wyler, Rich. "A Change of Heart: My Two Years in Reparative Therapy," People Can Change, 2010. http://peoplecanchange.com /stories/rich.php.

Websites

Amplify Your Voice (www.amplifyyourvoice.org). A project of Advocates for Youth, this website features blog entries, videos, news articles, and personal stories about sexual orientation, contraception, self-harm, and other critical issues.

It Gets Better Project (www.itgetsbetter.org). This website features videos of gay, lesbian, and straight adults sharing messages of hope and perseverance with LGBT children struggling with coming out, bullying, and other issues.

National Day of Silence (www.dayofsilence.org). This website organizes a national day of silence in schools across the country to bring attention to anti-LGBT name-calling, bullying, and harassment in schools.

The Safe Schools Coalition (www.safeschoolscoalition.org). This website offers resources to educators, parents, and guardians on how to make schools a safer place for gay, lesbian, and transgendered youth.

The Trevor Project (www.thetrevorproject.org). This website provides crisis intervention and suicide prevention services to lesbian, gay, bisexual, transgender, and questioning youth.

True Tolerance (www.truetolerance.org). This site, run by the family values group Focus on the Family, argues against sexualizing education policies and antibullying programs.

Index

Hubley, Jamie, 7

I
It Gets Better Project, 7–8

J
Johnson, Aidan, 47
Johnston, Michael, 44
Journal of Adolescent Health, 7
Journal of Biosocial Science, 14
Jung, Carl 34

K
Kehoe, Christine, *61*
King, Martin Luther, Jr.
Kinsey, Alfred, 12, 37–38

L
LaBarbera, Peter, 8
Lambda Legal, 7
Latham, Tyger, 80
Leno, Mark, 60, 61, *61*, 63
LGBT (lesbian/gay/bisexual/
   transgendered) community
   college graduation/income
      levels in, 76, 77
   does not need more legal
      rights, 75–79
   needs more legal rights,
      70–74
LGBT issues
   should be taught in schools,
      59–63
   should not be taught in
      schools, 64–68
Liberty Education Forum, 17
Los Angeles Times (newspaper),
   43, 64

Lucas, Billy, 7

M
Mattachine Society, 77
Matthew Shepard Foundation,
   72. *See also* Shepard, Matthew
McGreevy, Patrick, 64
Medved, Michael, 11
Melonakos, Kathleen, 55
Military
   countries allowing service by
      openly gay people, in, *99*
   should let soldiers be open
      about sexual orientation,
      89–94
   should not let soldiers be open
      about sexual orientation,
      95–101

N
National Association for
   Research & Therapy of
   Homosexuality, 55
National Center for Health
   Statistics, 12, 88
National Center for
   Transgender Equality, 71
National Conference of State
   Legislatures, 86
National Gay and Lesbian Task
   Force, 71
Nicolosi, Joseph, 31, 32– 38,
   41–42
NORC (University of Chicago),
   73–74

O
Obama, Barack, 90–91, *91,* 94

Picture Credits